# MILLER'S

## COLLECTING
## BLUE & WHITE
## POTTERY

# COLLECTING
# BLUE & WHITE
# POTTERY

## Gillian Neale

# Miller's Collecting Blue & White Pottery
## Gillian Neale

First published in Great Britain in 2004 by Miller's,
an imprint of Octopus Publishing Group Ltd,
2–4 Heron Quays, London, E14 4JP

Miller's is a registered trademark of Octopus Publishing Group Ltd

| | |
|---|---|
| **Senior Executive Editor** | Anna Sanderson |
| **Executive Art Editor** | Rhonda Fisher |
| **Editor** | Catherine Emslie |
| **Page Design** | SteersMcGillan Ltd |
| **Senior Designer** | Victoria Bevan |
| **Proofreader** | Barbara Mellor |
| **Indexer** | Sue Farr |
| **Production** | Sarah Rogers |
| **Special Photography** | Steve Tanner, Roy Farthing, A.J. Photographics |
| **Picture Research** | Nick Wheldon |

The publishers will be grateful for any information that will assist them in keeping future editions up to date. While every care has been taken in the preparation of this book, neither the author nor the publisher can accept any liability for any consequence arising from the use thereof, or the information contained therein.

Values should be used as a guide only, as prices vary according to geographical location and demand. US prices have been calculated at a rate of 1.5.

**ISBN 1 84000 833 4**

A CIP record for this book is available from the British Library

Set in Granjon and Helvetica
Produced by Toppan Printing Co., (HK) Ltd.
Printed and bound in China

**Front of jacket:** Rare five-part ice pail by Davenport, in the "Chinoiserie"-style "High Bridge" pattern, *c.*1815, £3,000–4,000/$4,500–6,000 (*see* page 97)

**Back of jacket, from left to right:** A rare Stilton bell by Spode, in the "Italian" pattern, *c.*1820, £2,000–2,500/$3,000–3,750 (*see* page 120); A jug printed in pink, *c.*1830, in the "Feeding the Turkeys" pattern, maker unknown, £250–300/$375–450 (*see* page 140)

**Half-title page:** Soup tureen stand by Jones, from the "British History" series, showing "The Seven Bishops to the Tower", *c.*1826–8, £550–650/$825–975 (*see* page 55)

**Title page:** Small-size ewer and bowl by Rogers, *c.*1810–15, showing the "Zebra" pattern, £750–900/$1,125–1,350 (*see* page 36)

# Contents

**6 Collecting Blue & White Pottery**

9    How and why it was made
14   History of Blue & White
16   Development of Design
20   Forming a Collection
24   Themes for Collecting

**26 Collecting by Design**

26   The Chinese Influence
28   Italian Influence: Spode
30   The "Italian" pattern: non-Spode
32   The "Wild Rose" border series
34   Export Wares
38   Flow Blue
40   Later patterns

**42 Collecting by Decoration**

42   The "Crown, Acorn, & Oak Leaf"
      border series
44   The "Bluebell" & "Foliage"
      border series
46   The "Tulip" & "Pineapple"
      border series
48   The "Grapevine" Border Series &
      other serial patterns
50   Cities & Towns: London
52   Other Cities & Towns
54   Historical Subjects
56   The Orient
58   Animals & Birds
64   Sporting Subjects
66   Armorial Designs
70   Floral Designs

**74 Collecting by Factory**

76   Spode
80   Minton

82   Wedgwood
84   Ridgway
86   Davenport
88   Riley & Rogers
90   Enoch Wood & the Adams Family
92   Masons & other Ironstone China

**94 Collecting by Use**

94    Dinnerware
98    Dessertware
100   Supper & Breakfast
104   Tea Wares
110   Children's & Nursery Items
114   Tureens
116   Drainers & Strainers
118   Cheese Dishes
122   Jugs
124   Pickle Dishes
126   Spoons & Ladles
128   Unusual Objects
132   Toiletware & Medical Items

**138 Other Colours**

138   Green
140   Puce, Mauve, & Pink
142   Brown, Black, & Orange

144   Display
146   Labels
147   Care & Repair
149   Pottery Marks

151   Glossary
153   Further Reading
154   Index
160   Acknowledgments

# Collecting Blue
# & White Pottery

▲ **A platter by Leeds Pottery, *c*.1800–10** The "Long Bridge" pattern. £150–200/$225–300

Collecting blue-and-white pottery, as with any other collecting, can be a time-consuming and yet extremely satisfying experience. Blue transfer-printed pottery (which is what this book deals with) has always been of interest to collectors, owing to the wide variety of patterns available and the vast range in prices, some of the rare specialist pieces reaching very high prices indeed.

The heyday for the manufacture of blue printed pottery was the early part of the nineteenth century, with the great Staffordshire potters producing it in vast quantities, particularly in the area around Stoke-on-Trent. Because of this it is sometimes referred to as "Staffordshire Blue"; another name is

"Blue Willow", an allusion to the original willow pattern – a copy of a Chinese design.

The extensive choice of patterns available adds much interest to collecting. They range from "Chinoiserie" – direct imitation of the Chinese style – to exotic animals and birds. These influences and images were brought back by people who had travelled to India or the Ottoman Empire. Most sons from the well-to-do middle class families either travelled or joined the army to further their education, before returning home to take a wife and start a family.

A very popular design to collect is the Spode "Indian Sporting" series produced around 1815, all based on a series of prints by Captain Williamson. These all depict the hunting and killing of various wild animals in the jungle.

Another popular design is the "Caramanian" series, also by Spode. This has an architectural theme, inspired by Near Eastern territories such as Egypt, and other countries that were part of the Ottoman Empire. Both of these Spode patterns share the same border.

Around 1820–5, views of English country houses, rural scenes, abbeys, churches, and cathedrals became popular. Slightly later, in the 1830s, views of Europe, particularly Italy, were in vogue.

▲ **An ale mug, *c*.1820**
Unknown maker; showing "The Crossing".
£350–400/$525–600

▲ **A plate in the rare "Durham Ox" pattern, *c*.1820**
Unknown maker. £450–550/$675–825

▲ **A pickle dish by Spode, *c*.1825**
In the "Filigree" pattern.
£175–225/$260–340

As for floral designs, the earliest were produced by Wedgwood in their "Botanical" series, the images for which were copied from William Curtis's *Botanical Magazine*. Spode and Minton also used floral patterns. The introduction of the Acts of Copyright in 1842 prevented the copying of designs from known engravings or paintings. During this period a more open, romantic, and stylized style was introduced. These items were less expensive, as the engraving was less intricate.

A collection may also be based around a manufacturer rather than a particular pattern. Spode is the most popular, but others are equally collectable: Wedgwood, Minton, Riley, Davenport, Rogers, Enoch Wood, and Adams to name a few.

So why collect? Firstly it should be a pleasure – an interesting hobby, a reason for going out and visiting places. It is also an opportunity to meet other like-minded collectors. It is rare, visiting an antiques fair or specialist auction, not to recognize a familiar face or two, and collecting can lead to lasting friendships.

I started collecting after being left a fruit bowl in the "Italian" pattern; I then toured the country looking for interesting items in the same pattern. From this a rather large collection developed. My

▲ **A pail-shaped custard cup by Spode, *c*.1820**
In the "Long Eliza" pattern.
£250–300/$375–450

▲ **A pub jug showing Litchfield Cathedral, *c*.1840**
Made for a pub in Haywards Heath,
Sussex. £350–400/$525–600

▲ **A jug by Enoch Wood, *c*.1820**
From the "Sporting" series, showing
"Shooting with Dogs".
£350–400/$525–600

enthusiasm led to my becoming a full-time specialist dealer in blue printed wares, but this beautiful pottery can be enjoyed at any level. Most collectors start in a very small way, buying the odd piece that takes their fancy. As we will see, the general direction of a collection often takes time to evolve, especially if it has no particular purpose, such as to fill a specific space in the home. At some stage a specialist dealer may be able to help with the thinning out of the unwanted pieces – either by buying them or by offering to sell them on a commission basis. There is no limit to the scope of collecting; with so much to learn it is up to the individual collector to decide the depth of research you want to do, how much money you are willing to spend, and how expansive you see your collection becoming. (*see* Forming a Collection, page 20, for further discussion on how to get started).

# How and why it was made

Blue-and-white transfer-printed pottery was originally produced in Staffordshire to satisfy the desire of the emerging middle classes to possess items of beauty for everyday use. The cost of imported porcelain from China, and to a lesser degree Europe, was prohibitive to all but the wealthiest. The pottery manufacturers centred around the Stoke-on-Trent area of Staffordshire, on the other hand, had a ready (and therefore cheap) supply of both labour and materials.

In the beginning they used local Staffordshire clay until they were able to ship a finer clay from Devon and Cornwall to Liverpool, and finally transport it by the Trent and Mersey canals to the potteries. To break it down, the clay is first allowed to weather on the factory site. This weathered clay is then formed into shapes using a plaster mould and both are placed into a drying oven. After some shrinkage the item can be separated from the mould and trimmed to size. It is then placed into "saggers" (racks) for firing in the biscuit oven. The biscuit coloured item is now ready for decoration.

## Transfer Printing

Transfer printing is a long and skilled process – especially the initial engraving of the copper plate, for which the engravers use a sharpened length of steel with a triangular head called the "graver". This has a mushroom-shaped wooden handle, which the engraver taps either by hand or using a small hammer. A small "V" shape is cut into the copper, the depth of the cut determining the intensity of the colour. A series of fine dot punching is used for the softer colour and background. The sharp edges are then removed using a steel scraper, and finally smoothed using a wet stone and water. This process known as "planishing", is necessary to allow the colour thoroughly to penetrate all the grooves in order to achieve a successful print.

Engraving a new copper plate took a minimum of six weeks to complete. It should be remembered, however, that in the early nineteenth century lighting was generally poor, and workers were unable to look after their eyes as well as we are today: working conditions did not encourage a speedy output. The smaller factories were often not able to employ their own engravers, so work was sent out – which may explain how some designs were copied. Today the process is largely unchanged, aside from the fact that the copper plates are coated with titanium to prolong the life of the plate. The disadvantage of this, however, is that some of the three-dimensional effect is lost.

When the copper plate is ready for use it is kept

▲ **A platter from the "Antique Scenery" series, c.1825** Showing Cathedral Church, Glasgow; with the accompanying source print. **Platter £550–650/$825–975 Print £250–300/$375–450**

▲ **Spode platter from the "Caramanian" series, *c*.1815**
Showing "Principal Entrance to the Harbour at Cacamo"; and the accompanying source print. **Platter £750–900/$1,125–1,350**
**Print £350–450/$525–675**

▲ **A copper plate used by Jamieson, *c*.1836-54, and the accompanying plate**
The "Gem" pattern. Although from the same series, is larger and therefore has a different centre. **Plate £40–60/$60–90**
**Copper plate £175–250/$260–375**

warm on a hot stove. The colour, in the form of an inorganic metallic oxide mixed with printing oil, is rubbed well into the grooves, using a wooden dabber. The excess is scraped off and finally wiped clean. Tissue paper is evenly applied to the copper plate with a soft soap solution. Both are then passed through a large press, the upper roller of which is covered with very thick felt, which forces the colour onto the paper.

Next the copper plate is returned to the stove, where the tissue is carefully removed and passed down the line to the "cutter", who cuts the necessary pieces required to decorate the item. These are passed to the transferrer, who applies the print and

smooths out all the creases. The tissue is kept in place by the oily texture of the mixture, while the print is forced onto the object using a stiff brush lubricated with soft soap.

Finally the item is placed in a bath of cold water for ten minutes, then the tissue is removed leaving the print intact. The transfer-printed item is inspected before entering the kiln for hardening, where it is fired at 680–750°C (1,256–1382°F) to fix the colour – which at this stage is not yet blue.

After hardening, the item is glazed and re-fired at 1050°C (1,922°F). It is at this stage that the colour turns blue, hence the name underglaze blue transfer-printed pottery.

1 **The copper plate and engraver's tools**
   The printng process begins with the engraving of a pattern onto a copper plate, a process that requires a great deal of skill.

2 **Dot punching**
   An engraving technique used to create softer shading and tonal variety over large areas.

3 **Using a "graver", or "burin"**
   This tool is used to engrave "V"-shaped grooves, which will contain the pigment.

4 **Applying the colour**
   The oxide and oil mixture is spread over the plate, which is heated at the same time over a hot stove. It is then rubbed well into the lines of the engraving, using a wooden "dabber" to make sure all grooves are filled.

5   **Removing excess colour**
Any excess dye is carefully scraped off.

6   **Eliminating final residue**
The scraper leaves a thin film, which is removed by bossing the copper with a cloth.

7   **The tissue paper**
After being wetted, or "sized", with a solution of soap and water, the tissue paper is laid on top of the copper plate.

8   **The press**
Both the paper and the copper plate now go through the press. Every part of the pattern is pressed onto the tissue paper by the upper roller, which is covered with felt.

9   **Separating plate and paper**
The print is carefully pulled away from the engraving, while the plate again rests on the hot stove.

10   **A "pull" from a copper plate**
An example of a print that has been pressed onto tissue paper, ready to be transferred to pottery.

**11 Cutting out sections**

The parts of the print required to fit the shapes of individual objects are cut out of the sheet of tissue paper.

**12 Applying the pattern**

The pieces of print are carefully placed in position by the transferrer. The paper is held in place by the tacky texture of the pigment.

**13 Transferring the pattern**

The print is transferred to the object by rubbing down on the tissue paper with a stiff-bristled brush lubricated with soap.

**14 Removing the paper**

The item is then immersed in cold water so that the tissue paper can be removed without damaging the colour.

**15 Inspection and firing**

Each item is rigourously inspected for any flaws before it enters the hardening-on kiln – at which stage the ink is not yet blue. The ware is fired at 680°–750°C (1,256–1,382°F), then glazed and re-fired at 1050°C (1,922°F) – when the design turns blue.

**16 A finished piece**

The pottery is now ready for final inspection.

# History of Blue & White

▲ **A Chinese "Nankin"-type dinner plate, *c.*1780–90**
Painted entirely by hand, an example of the style that the English potters copied. Items like this were originally imported to Europe in enormous quantities. **£50–80/$75–120**

▲ **Spode, Parasol & Figure, *c.*1810**
Transfer-printed plate; compare with hand-painted plate.
**£80–120/$120–180**

Blue pottery's introduction and use was dependent on many factors. From the early part of the eighteenth century the East India Company had been importing quantities of tea to England from China. To provide ballast for the ships, they also imported richly glazed hard-paste Chinese porcelain. This was all hand-painted directly on to the biscuit crust, glazed, and fired only once. It was very popular in the West, where it complemented the heavy style of oak furniture.

By the early nineteenth century however, tastes tended towards much lighter, paler colours and woods such as mahogany and walnut. The dark, heavyweight Chinese porcelain did not marry with this new look (even though designs would be based on the Chinese style – "Chinoiserie" – for a long time to come), so much less was imported. Spode was approached to cater to these new tastes, but the cost of hand-painting was prohibitive. Thus the transfer printing process evolved and was finally perfected.

Originally, tea imported from China carried very heavy import duties of 119 per cent, making it available only to the wealthy for use in their silver teapots. In 1784, however, the import duty on tea was reduced to 12½ per cent, at the same time as the duty on the sale of silver was reintroduced. Conveniently for blue-and-white pottery, the

ceramic teapot came to be very much in demand!

Wedgwood perfected a cream-coloured earthenware, "creamware", about 1770, on which he experimented with various forms of decoration. He then introduced "Pearlware" at the end of the 19th century, using higher proportions of Cornish clay to give a whiter appearance, with a small amount of cobalt added to the glaze to create the pearl effect. Spode introduced his stone china in 1805; and C.J. Mason was granted a patent for his "ironstone" china in 1813.

In 1820, factories tried adding a cup of lime or ammonia to the oven during the glazing process, which allowed the colour to run slightly, giving a softer outline. Known as "flow blue", this effect was arguably first discovered accidentally. It was extremely popular with the North American market, and since the 1960s has again become an American favourite due to its availability there.

The art of engraving had not been perfected at this stage – patterns were made up from lines rather than the dots of later production – and wares had a much darker, heavier appearance, with a lack of naturalistic shading, which improved over time. The process was also improved by the use of a finer moist paper, which was more pliable than the thick dry paper used in the original trials by the potter

▶ **A platter by Heath, c.1815** Showing the "Raindeer" pattern.
£250–350/$375–525

▼ **A plate by Turner, c.1790–1800** Showing an early line-engraved pattern with feather edging.
£175–225/$260–340

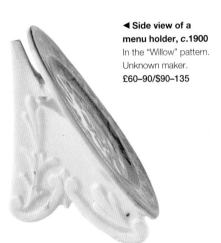

◀ **Side view of a menu holder, c.1900** In the "Willow" pattern. Unknown maker.
£60–90/$90–135

Badley. A new and revolutionary machine for the manufacture of finer and stronger tissue paper was developed by Fourdriner at a paper mill in Dartford, Kent (and later Hanley).

## The "Willow" Pattern Story

The classic "Willow" pattern was one of the first to be introduced, inspired by a Chinese legend in which the daughter of a wealthy Mandarin falls in love with one of her father's lowly employees. Their love is forbidden, and it is arranged that she will marry more respectably (the three figures on the bridge depict the two lovers being chased by the father). Eventually the girl's father catches them and the boy is killed, whereupon the girl goes to a house to which she sets fire, dying in the flames. The two lovers are reunited in death as two love birds. Close inspection of the "Willow" pattern reveals every element of the legend, including the flames shooting from the burning building. The exact origin of the tale is uncertain but it lends great charm to the design. Many other potters went on to produce this pattern, now recognized worldwide, though none was to rival Spode. There were also slight variations in the design – for instance, in some there are only two figures on the bridge, and in "Long Bridge" pattern the bridge is longer.

Blue-and-white pottery flourished as a result of the middle class prosperity created by the Industrial Revolution, and the revival of the trade after 1815, which saw the end of the Napoleonic wars and the signing of the Peace Treaty with America.

# Development of Design

As we have seen, the earliest patterns were all copies of Chinese designs (though the study of the Chinese-type pattern is a field of its own and beyond the scope of this book). They were often then altered to include a variety of different motifs, such as the "Buffalo" pattern, which shows a boy ridding a buffalo in a Chinese-style landscape design. Several factories produced this design, the most sought-after being by Spode. The pattern remains very dark in colour, as it is line-engraved rather than being of the later "stippling" variety.

Another very prolific design was the "Chinoiserie Ruins" pattern produced by Davenport, called the "Hermit" pattern when made by Minton. This is a very intricate design showing a Chinese landscape and ruins. This time the pattern is lighter in colour, as it is stipple-engraved rather than line. Many variations on the standard "Willow" pattern appeared – some without the bridge. The number of figures on these varies, as does the number of pagodas.

In 1805, Spode and Herculaneum produced the "Flying Pennant" pattern, which is much lighter, with a more open and distinctive border. It is characterized by the boat in the foreground with a prominent pennant or flag flying from the mast. The pattern is rarely marked, and there are only minor variations in the style of engraving between the factories.

Further variations on the Chinese theme were the "Elephant" and "Zebra" patterns produced by Rogers, showing the animals in a slightly incon-gruous Chinese landscape. The two patterns both have a wide border of large flowers and a much more defined picture. Both became very popular, the "Zebra" especially so with the North American market – an example with a rare export mark can be seen on page 37 – and today it is equally as popular in Briatin as in America.

The "Net" pattern produced by Spode and other factories again has a Chinese influence. Pagodas and willow trees in medallions form the inner border; the centre has a net decoration with a floral cross in the middle; and the outer border contains a similar pattern. Variations occur between the factories – mainly in the central cross. Very few of the examples are marked, most attributions being based on shape and the quality of the potting.

The next stage in the development of design was triggered by the young gentlemen of the upper class, who – in order to complete their wordly education before settling down – either went into the army or embarked on the "Grand Tour" which embraced Europe, especially Italy, and sometimes India and the Ottoman Empire. As they came back with tales of their adventures and animals they had seen, so the demand for more exotic patterns that echoed these ideas increased.

Spode introduced a design called the "Caramanian" series around 1810, showing many different views of scenes in the East. Most of these views were taken from Luigi Mayer's aquatints entitled *Views in Egypt, Palestine, and the Ottoman*

▲ **Lid of a supper set segment by Davenport,**
**c.1815** In the "Chinoiserie Ruins" pattern.
£60–80/$90–120

▲ **Teapot stand, c.1820**
By Barker, of the Don pottery partnership.
£190–220/$285–330

and the "Parrot" border showing views of India, both produced by Ridgway.

Views of Europe, and in particular Italy, were popular; patterns such as the "Italian", "Tower", "Castle", and "Bridge of Lucano" by Spode were very prized – and most of these patterns (again, especially the "Italian") continued being produced well into the late twentieth century.

Around 1820 people's tastes changed again, as the popularity of blue-and-white continued to grow. Potters' agents visited large towns selling wares to retailers, who in turn demanded exclusive rights to certain patterns in their area.

New designs evolved, of country houses and stately homes, churches, cathedrals, and other such imposing buildings. Most of these were serial patterns sharing a distinctive border, with the central picture changing depending on the

▲ **Jug, *c*.1800–1810**
Showing "Boy on Buffalo" pattern; with extensive restoration to the spout, which affected its value by a third. **£40–50/$60–75**

*Empire*, published in 1803. This was to become the first serial pattern printed on pottery – in which the design changed with each different shape of pottery – and it was very popular. The pattern was very intricate, requiring great skill both in the engraving and the fitting of the transfer to the item. The plates had an indented edge to the rim, making the correct alignment of the pattern essential. Later on, however, the items became less intricately shaped.

The next serial pattern introduced by Spode was the famous and very popular "Indian Sporting" series. The source for this was the artist Samuel Howitt's drawings entitled *Oriental Field Sports* (along with Captain Thomas Williamson's manuscript). This pattern, as its name suggests, shows Eastern big game hunting scenes featuring animals native to the region such as elephants and tigers – a collectors' field in itself. Both this pattern and the "Caramanian" share the same border of animals, which seems more appropriate to the sporting series. These two patterns provided inspiration for a whole new trend in pottery decoration. Views of India were copied from engravings by the famous William and Thomas Daniell, with some patterns composed from parts of several engravings. These were made by potters such as Herculaneum, Rogers, and Riley, to name only a few. Other patterns were the "Ottoman Empire" series showing views of Asia,

▲ **Pierced basket and stand by Spode, *c*.1815–20**
In the "Flying Pennant" pattern. **£400–550/$600–825**

▲ **A pair of knife rests by Henshall, *c*.1825–30**
Showing the border from the "Castle and Bridge" pattern.
**£225–275/$335–415 pair**

▲ **A cusped dessert dish by Spode,** *c.*1815–20
Showing the "Net" pattern. **£160–240/$240–360**

individual object. The amount of engraving involved was enormous – each service was created using upwards of a dozen different copper plates. This type of pattern was introduced in 1820–5. Most of the designs are referred to by their border, the "Grapevine" border by Enoch Wood or the "Crown, Acorn & Oak Leaf" border by Meir for example. Carey produced the "Cathedral" series, showing various British cathedrals such as St Paul's, York, Litchfield, Chichester, Bath, and Bristol; this has a very distinctive border with a design reminiscent of a bishop's mitre. Carey also produced a series called "Irish Scenery", despite the fact that not all the views are of Ireland – one in fact shows Warwick Castle in the Midlands.

Many single patterns were also produced, the "Beemaster" being particularly famous. This was copied from an oil painting called *The Swarm of Bees in Autumn* by George Robertson; the original painting of the same name is now in the Cecil Higgins Art Gallery, Bedford. The potter for this design is unknown, but it is possible that two separate factories may have produced it – a likely explanation given the two different standards of potting, and of setting of the transfer, across a whole group of items in this pattern. Two other unattributed but desirable patterns are the "Winemakers" and the "Grazing Rabbits".

Also produced at this time was the "Durham Ox" series depicting shorthorn cattle, the maker of

which is unkown. The poor overfed ox of the title was trailed around fat stock shows in England and Scotland until it eventually died. This design is highly collectable and commands very high prices especially at auction. Another rural scene produced was the "Gamekeeper", which until recently remained unattributed – but a plate has now been found bearing the name Hackwood.

In 1805, Wedgwood produced a wonderful series called the "Botanical". The images were accurate copies from William Curtis's *Botanical Magazine*, which was quite a departure from the traditional style – a very simple border of small circles with a single plant in the centre, seeming comparitively modern. The early ones have small numbers at the base referring to the print from which the design was taken. Wedgwood also produced other floral designs, including "Waterlily", "Peony", and "Hibiscus" – the latter having a Chinese feel to the border. Other factories soon produced floral patterns (*see* Floral Designs, page 70) – Spode and Minton being particularly prolific. They also introduced the look of white on blue rather than blue on white, created by increasing the depths of the cut into the copper plate during the engraving process.

A new type of design, called a sheet pattern, was developed around 1830. As the name suggests, a sheet of wallpaper-like design was cut to fit the object, giving an all-over pattern. It is often possible to see the joins in the design, revealing some of the method of transfer printing.

Between 1826 and 1828, Jones of Hanley produced a range called "British History", another serial pattern. The plates and soup plates are fairly

▲ **A dog dish by Spode,**
*c.*1820
Showing the "Tower" pattern.
**£800–950/$1,200–1,425**

▲ **A 30cm (12in) charger by Edward & George Phillips,**
*c.1828–34* Showing the "Park Scenery" pattern. These large
round chargers are difficult to find. **£250–300/$375–450**

These patterns were also mass-produced, and so the quality on the whole was poor. None the less, a decline in production was triggered, with only the well-known potters surviving using their original patterns. A lot of this inferior pottery was exported, until the market became saturated and the sales decreased. Then other countries began to produce their own wares, reducing still further the demand for export.

Many of the Spode-registered patterns continued well up to the end of the nineteenth century, and some of the original patterns are being reproduced today using copies of the original copper plates held at the Spode factory. As can be imagined, these modern reproductions no longer have the same three-dimensional effect after the plates have been coated with titanium to make them last longer. At some time, however, these also may very well become collectors' items.

sible that very few were produced. An interesting mark naming the battle or scene commemorated is always found on the reverse of the item.

Another collectable series that was developed is the "College Views" series by Ridgway, showing the various Oxford and Cambridge colleges.

Many designs were also produced exclusively for the North American market, commemorating battles, historical events, and places such as New York's City Hall, St Paul's Church Boston, Court House Boston, Boston Almshouse, and the Baltimore Exhange, by Ridgway, and Boston State House, by Rogers, all produced between 1820 and 1830. Thomas Mayer also produced the "Arms of America" series, showing the arms of various states. Dark blue was preferred by the American export market, but in the late 1820s experiments began with other colours – notably brown, black, green, and puce. These colours were eventually perfected and much of this pottery was exported.

The passing by parliament in 1842 of the Registration of Design Act had a detrimental effect on the designs of patterns. Before this act, the laws of copyright were very loosely followed; now, by contrast, the copying of prints, paintings, or other people's designs was prohibited. From this position more open, romantic designs evolved, with exotic names bearing no resemblance to the pattern. The patterns had much more white and less pattern, making them easier to produce. The colour was paler and less dramatic in appearance.

▲ **A soup plate by Ridgway,**
*c.1825*
From the "British Flowers"
series. **£140–190/$210–285**

# Forming a Collection

◀ **A very desirable platter, *c*.1820**
By an unknown maker; showing the "Durham Ox & John Day". These platters are making high prices at auction.
**£5,000–6,000/ $7,500–9,000**

Collecting anything is a very personal thing. Most collections are started purely by chance, or at least are not planned down to the last object. They evolve naturally, often changing direction, as one gains more knowledge and becomes aware of the huge choice available. However, the first purchase is often the most treasured, long after the theme of the collection has changed direction or pieces of more monetary value have been acquired.

A collection could start with a family item, a change in the interior design of the home, or a piece of furniture that needs decorating or filling. Home interior magazines often show dresser, cabinet, or wall displays of blue-and-white china. Ideas are endless. Ask yourself why you want to collect, where your treasures are to be displayed, and most importantly how much you can afford to spend. A hobby can turn into a full-time business – so beware!

There are many different sources of blue-and-white items; from car-boot and garage sales – if you are very lucky or eagle-eyed – to one-day antiques fairs (not always selling priceless antiques), to auctions holding ceramic sales and often specialized blue-and-white sales. The Internet, with on-line auctions or dealers' websites, has become an increasingly valuable arena for buying, selling,

and research. Another source is antiques shops; most have some blue-and-white, if only to decorate the furniture.

Buying from a quality antiques fair, where all the stock is vetted by experts and is therefore guaranteed as genuine, is highly recommended – as is buying from specialist dealers who have a depth

▲ **A small advertising plate, *c*.1840**
In the "Willow" pattern; showing "Yorkshire Relish Thick or Thin"; other inscriptions exist in the series. **£30–50/$45–75**

▲ **The author on her stand at the Olympia Fine Art and Antiques Fair**
Showing a Davenport vegetable tureen to a collector. Antique fairs boast an extraordinary wealth of choice, combined with expertise.

of knowledge of the subject and usually a passionate interest that will rub off on you. Using a specialist will give the collector the benefit of experience as well as access to a large and varied stock

Buying from a car-boot or garage sale can be great fun, and very occasionally bargains do appear. When doing this you are relying on your own knowledge as to whether a piece is genuine. Most of the sellers know what they are doing, and many are often professional "booters" moving from one sale to another. The experienced buyer gets there very early and watches the seller unpack – be shrewd. The seller will expect to be paid in cash.

Some of the one-day fairs can be a good hunting ground, but again be aware that everything is not always as described. Ask for a detailed receipt mentioning any damage or repairs. A refusal to do this should always arouse your suspicions.

There are many massive outdoor showground fairs, some with up to three thousand stalls. Many very good dealers stand at these fairs because of the enormous through-put of buyers. As you may imagine, it is easy to get lost and forget where you saw something. The best advice is: if you see something you like at a price you are prepared to pay, buy it: you may not find the stall again and if you do the item may have gone. These very large

fairs are very exhausting and often held in cold windy isolated spots with very little shelter from the elements between buildings. Go prepared with raincoat, boots, and large bags to carry any treasures. And remember where the car is!

The Internet is becoming a very popular source of supply, but it is not a personal service. The best way to learn about pottery is to handle it and get the feel. Learn to check for any repairs or alterations. Ceramic restoration is now very skilled; handles, knobs, and even lids can be replaced. Pay particular attention to the border pattern, as repaired chips will be hand-painted with a brush, so the outline is not so fine. Experience will eventually give you confidence in checking for restorations.

Using the Internet allows you to buy worldwide from the comfort of your own home, without the need to travel. This is not without dangers – not everyone is honest in their descriptions. When buying this way it is advisable to pay by credit card, as opposed to cheque, as this gives a degree of consumer protection. On-line auctions can again be very tempting, but the item is only viewable in a photograph; and auctions may occur at odd times, often at night, so bidding is not always convenient. Most auction sites provide a degree of protection and consumer cover for purchases. Another pitfall

**▲ A warming dish, c.1820**
Showing the rare "Winemakers"
pattern. Maker unknown.
£350–450/$525–675

**▲ A warming dish by
Spode, c.1820**
Showing the "Tower" pattern.
£200–250/$300–375

lies in the sending of purchased goods, usually by post, which is only as reliable as the person who packs the item. Always obtain insurance cover.

Buying from auction can be very exciting, but always inspect the goods carefully before the sale. There is usually a viewing day prior to the sale, although not always on the actual day of the sale – unfortunately damage may occur between the viewing and the time of the sale. Decide on an item you like and set yourself an upper limit that you are prepared to pay, bearing in mind the buyer's premium of anything from eight to twenty per cent. Listen to the auctioneer carefully and be sure that he or she sees your bid. Be very strong-minded and do not get carried away, otherwise you could pay much more than you intended. At the fall of the hammer it is too late to change your mind: you have entered into an agreement to pay that price. Go armed with wrapping paper and some means of carrying the items home, as not all auction houses supply packing.

Forming a good relationship with a specialist dealer is often the best way to source items for your collection. Advice can be sought, special items sourced, and mistakes often exchanged. Some dealers inform collectors of items that become available which may be of interest to them, and send invitations to visit antique fairs.

Having discovered the various methods of sourcing items for your collection, you should consider the direction that it is going to take. If the idea is to fill a dresser, make sure always to carry with you the size of the shelves, including the width between them: nothing is more disappointing than getting home to find that a plate will not fit! It is probably best to decide what theme, factory, or even which tone of blue to start with. Alternatively, you can collect all the same pattern. It is usually better to

find the "background" to the collection first, composed of larger, flat items such as plates, platters, or dishes, and then fill in the foreground with the small items later. Many a collector has exhausted all their space and moved on to another room; the advantage here is that all blue-and-white pottery can be mixed together – this even adds to its charm (see Display, pages 144–5). On starting out, some collectors buy every piece they see, later becoming much more focused and sticking to one theme or factory.

Reading specialist books and magazines is a great aid to learning (see Further Reading, page 153). Local reference libraries are usually very helpful and will readily order in a book if requested. If you find an item which cannot be identified from

**▲ A Spode soup plate,
c.1825**
In the "Botanical" pattern.
£160–190/$240–285

▲ **A smoker's set printed in brown, by Middlesborough Pottery, c.1840** In the "Calodonia" pattern. It is very rare to find one complete with the tamper, which is used to weight the tobacco in the jar. **£550–750/$825–1,125**

any book, it is worth asking a specialist dealer if they can help with the research: most are only too happy to do so.

There are various clubs and societies for collectors, which encourage the sharing of enthusiasm for the subject as well as the exchanging of information that may lead to more discoveries. The specialist club in England for blue-and-white is "Friends of Blue", while in America there is the "Transferware Collectors Club" and the "Flow Blue International Collector's Club". There is also the "Spode Society", which covers all Spode ceramics, rather than just blue-and-white transferware, and can be a rich source of information (*see* right).

## Collectors' Clubs
## Friends of Blue and other Clubs & Societies

The "Friends of Blue", or FOB as it is known, was started in 1973. The first meeting was held at the Victoria and Albert Museum, London, attracting visitors from around the world. Identification of many patterns from their source prints has been researched by some of the founder members.

A quarterly bulletin is published with members submitting articles for inclusion, and also photographs of new acquisitions. This frequently leads to much discussion; meetings are often held at member's homes where they exhibit their collections with great pride.

An Annual General Meeting is held in the potteries area of Staffordshire on the last Sunday in June, where speakers talk on various aspects of collecting. A blue table is prepared here where members can bring items for sale or exchange.

In 1998, to celebrate their twenty-fifth anniversary, an exhibition of items from members collections was displayed at the Wedgwood Museum. A catalogue was also produced which provides a useful reference tool. The Friends of Blue also have a website, www.fob.org.uk, which contains interesting and useful information.

The American "Transferware Collectors' Club" is run on similar lines, and sometimes travels to Stoke-on-Trent for its annual meeting. Details are available from www.merlinantiques.com, or go straight to www.transcollectorsclub.org. More specifically concentrating on the "flow blue" variety of blue-and-white pottery is the American "Flow Blue International Collector's Club", which can be found at www.flowblue.org.

The "Spode Society" deals with all aspects of ceramic collecting, including porcelain, and offers many interesting articles and lectures on blue-and-white pottery. The main Spode website is www.spode.co.uk. There is also a Spode museum in Stoke-on-Trent, which includes a very interesting "Blue Room" devoted entirely to early Spode blue-and-white wares – well worth a visit. In addition, you may of course discover local antiques clubs with ceramic sections – or you could always start a new one.

# Themes for Collecting

Choosing a theme allows you to steer your collection in a certain direction, and enhances the satisfaction that it provides. Some collectors buy everything in sight when they first start, only later learning to narrow down their purchases. It is better not just to search for the rare and unusual, as by their very nature these are difficult to find, so your interest is likely to diminish fairly rapidly.

Always buy the best that you can afford – in perfect condition if possible. For rarer items this is not always possible: because most of these things were in everyday use, the fewer surviving examples of an item there are, the less chance there is of finding one that has not been damaged by natural wear and tear. None the less, always aim for high standards and you will build a collection to be proud of. This book will help demonstrate just what is available, so helping you to build the collection you want.

The theme will be dictated by your personal choice as well as by any financial and spatial restrictions. There are so many options to choose from. Collecting by factory is as good a choice as any. Spode, for instance, probably has the widest variety of patterns to choose from and the quality of production is always good and the engraving and the placing of the transfer can not be faulted.

Another way of theming your collection is to choose one pattern, for example the "Willow", and hunt only for examples of this. Many people start this way, as it makes it possible to focus on finding new shapes and sizes, so providing a pleasing variety to the eye: all being in one pattern, they of course blend together very well and provide a fine display.

Collecting by use – that is, by what the object *is*, rather than what pattern it is in or what factory it comes from – is a very interesting approach. Going down this route may mean that it will take much longer to increase the size of your collection, but it is particularly fascinating as there are so many different shapes to concentrate on. Many collectors focus on medical and nursery items such as chamber pots, baby bottles, and eye baths, for example.

People have been known to make up a harlequin dinner service in, for example, floral designs, which can then be used on special occasions. It is quite possible to mix up items of a similar design that are not of the same pattern or by the same manufacturer: florals lend themselves particularly well to this as they are fairly fluid in line, and it helps if the shade of blue is similar. If you actually use the

▲ **A giant-size punch bowl by Keeling, in the "Lakeside Meeting" pattern, *c.*1825** Printed on one side is "H. Adams Crown Inn", possibly indicating it was special commission for this inn. **£2,000-plus/$3,000-plus, in perfect condition**

items you collect, their personal value increases immeasurably, and they all look very attractive displayed on a dresser when not in use.

Collecting large items such as meat platters and drainers can be an expensive hobby, but they look particularly impressive displayed on a plate shelf around a room, or fixed to a wall using fine nylon thread, which is invisible when in place. I know of a palace overseas where the walls in one room are decorated entirely with drainers and pierced plates. They are in fact set in plaster, meaning they can never be removed – not something to be recommended. Jugs come in innumerable shapes and sizes from the miniature in a toy service to a very large footbath jug. It is very important for jugs to be perfect and

**▼ A pilgrim flask by the Don Pottery, Yorkshire, *c.*1830**
A very rare item, showing the "Vermicelli" pattern.
The reverse (below) shows an inscripion of the owner's initials.
£1,500–2,000/$2,250–3,000

**▲ A plate in the "Beemaster" pattern, *c.*1820**
A rare pattern by an as yet unknown maker.
£250–325/$375–490

unrestored if they are to be used, as restoration will not resist prolonged contact with water.

Another "use" to collect by could be children's or miniature china. This would be good for a collector with little space to spare – small objects do not take up much room and are best displayed in a glass cabinet. There are some very interesting miniatures, but bear in mind that they were played with by children, so are often damaged. Complete services can be bought in one group, or compiled by collecting each piece individually. Prices may appear high in comparison to larger items, but it should be remembered that not only were they easily lost by their child owners, but also fewer were produced, and small items sometimes required intricate work.

Tea wares are another option: cups, saucers, coffee cans, tea and coffee pots, cream jugs, and sucriers are just some of the items to be found that were used in the consumption of that all-important beverage without which blue-and-white pottery would surely never have been produced in such large quantities, or developed to such an extent.

Collecting other colours of transfer-printed pottery is growing in popularity all the time. A theme can be continued into non-blue – as with the "Aesop's Fables" series by Spode, or the "Byron's Views" series by Copeland and Garrett, for example. Although both of these patterns were made in blue using the same copper plates, their general appearance is very different when produced in green, brown, or black. Some collectors have a blue room, a green room, and so on.

Collecting by pattern, design, and decoration can become as specific or broad as you like. For example, rather than just collecting one particular pattern, you could choose a subject into which several patterns may fall. Whatever your decision, the choice is endless – rural scenes, country houses, or historical scenes; Eastern, American, or European views; animals, birds, and flowers – almost every subject was reproduced on printed pottery.

The best advice is to buy what pleases you most (while having some sort of focus), what you can afford, and what you will enjoy sharing your home with. You will inevitably make mistakes when choosing what to buy, but most can be rectified – and we all learn by experience.

# Collecting by Design

Trace the development of blue & white – from archetypal patterns to eclectic later styles

**▲ A pickle dish by Davenport, *c*.1815–20**
Showing the "Bisham Abbey" pattern, also known as "Tudor Mansion". £195–245/$290–370

**▶ A square salad bowl by Spode, *c*.1820**
Showing "The Flying Pennant" pattern.
£250–350/$375–525

# The Chinese Influence

All blue-and-white pottery owes its origins to Chinese designs, or to "Chinoiserie" – the term signifying the European adoption of all things Chinese, which developed into a fanciful notion of China, using stylized, exaggerated motifs.

Generally speaking, the "Chinoiserie" designs are less expensive than other patterns, the reason being that they may appear less interesting on a superficial level. But closer study of the patterns reveals that they are often very beautiful. Most contain some type of landscape, pagodas, trees, and water; some have birds, boats, and figures.

The Chinese designs often date back to the end of the eighteenth century, so the colour is a much darker blue, owing both to the instability of the colour and the coarser engraving of the copper plate. The colour of the "Willow" pattern can vary, from the attractive medium blue of both Spode and Wedgwood patterns to the darker heavier designs of the lesser Staffordshire potters. There are also some interesting shapes, especially

in hollow-ware such as tea- or coffee pots.

The "Broseley", or "Temple", pattern is similar in design to the "Willow", having a willow tree and two men on a bridge, but is very much paler and even indistinct. It is more usually found on tea wares, and often with gilded edges: care should be taken to not rub this away through use, as this devalues it. Spode also used the pattern for dinner and dessert items. Quality varies a great deal between manufacturers, Spode and Mile Mason being the best. An interesting theme on which to focus might be all the "Willow"-type patterns without a bridge, produced by several factories. Davenport called it the "Bridgeless Willow", and Minton named it the "Hermit" pattern, after the lone figure in the temple doorway.

Another Chinese-derived landscape design by Spode is the "Forest Landscape", which as the name implies is an all-over pattern of trees, a pagoda, and an island – a very attractive, if busy, pattern. The colour is paler than some designs as

◄ **A coffee pot by Stevenson, *c.*1815**
In the "Chinoiserie High Bridge" pattern.
£250–300/$375–450

▲ **A soup plate by Spode, *c.*1805** In the "Grasshopper" pattern. This pattern was usually used on stone china, as the backstamp on this piece indicates.
£80–110/$120–165

► **A plate by Hamilton, *c.*1815–20**
Showing the "Canton Views" pattern.
£90–130/$135–195

it was produced in the very early part of the nineteenth century. The "Buffalo" pattern shows a boy riding a buffalo in a Chinese landscape. It was made by many factories, but a piece marked Spode is a great find.

If landscape designs are not your favoured subject, there are other patterns with a Chinese feel. The "Grasshopper", produced in 1805 by Spode, one of the few Spode transfer-printed patterns produced on stone china (the backstamp includes the words "New Stone"), shows a typical "Willow"-type border of Chinese symbols: a fence, a vase of Chinese flowers, and two insects – one of which is the grasshopper. A slightly later version of this, made around 1820, has a different border of flowers, the same as the border from Spode's "Group" pattern. The latter is more difficult to find and not always printed on stone china, though it is arguably more attractive.

The "Net" pattern, produced by factories such as Herculaneum, Ridgway, and Spode, has a central net design with pagodas and willow trees in medallions around it. The pattern covers the whole object, so can appear rather busy. It is interesting to compare the work of different factories, noting the subtle variations in style.

Another very prolific design is the "Chinese Trophies" pattern, again produced by many factories. This depicts arms and helmets, revealing fascinating detail on close inspection. It can be divided into three sections: the "Trophies Dagger" (the original and earliest), the "Trophies Nankin", and the "Trophies Etruscan", also known as the "Hundred Antiquities". The last is often clobbered with red and yellow.

There are many other patterns with a Chinese influence – either fantastical "Chinoiserie" designs or even reproductions of actual landscapes such as that of the Canton River, as in the plate above. A collection can easily evolve from this theme, and it may lead on to other patterns as you develop a taste for landscape, nature, or stories.

◀ **A shell dessert comport dish by Spode,**
***c*.1820–5** Showing the "Tower" pattern.
£170–225/$255–340

▶ **A shell dessert comport
dish by Spode, *c*.1815**
Showing the "Castle" pattern.
£175–240/$260–360

# Italian Influence: Spode

Some of the most popular and best-loved designs by Spode have a very definite Italian influence – and none more so than the famous "Italian" pattern itself. A very enduring pattern, it was first produced in 1818 and is still made today. The origins of the pattern are unclear, but it may be that elements of it derive from an unsigned pencil sketch (or sketches) copied from a Claude Lorraine pastoral landscape of 1638, which is in Parham House, Sussex.

As the design was so popular, it can be found on almost every kind of object. Some very interesting shapes exist, especially from the late nineteenth and early twentieth centuries, including quite large and attractive vases and urns. Umbrella stands, toilet wares, and toy sets are all available – not forgetting a vast array of tea wares. Two items of particular interest to be found are an octagonal sandwich plate with a raised cross in the centre, which was obtained in exchange for coupons from Skipper sardine tins, and the "Melba"-shape fruit bowl available with coupons from Sunlight soap, offers

for which were available between 1934 and 1946.

The "Castle" pattern, or "Gate of San Sebastian", is the earliest of the designs to be taken from a series of aquatints by Merigot – *Views of Rome and the Vicinity*, published in 1796–8 – probably introduced in 1806. The pattern is dominated by a large gateway, a drover with cattle in the foreground, and a river to the right of the picture, with people crossing a bridge over the water. It is of a lighter blue than the other designs of the time. Tureens in this pattern were made in two shapes, the earliest examples being oval and the later ones, after 1825, square with small feet. These were produced in huge quantities and also copied by other factories, notably Clews and Swansea. The Clews examples are usually marked, while the Swansea pattern's blue has a greenish tint to it and often a fine white edge to the border.

The "Tower" pattern was among the most popular designs after the "Italian". Its source print (also from Merigot) depicts the Bridge of Salaro, near

▲ **A dessert basket by Spode,**
*c.*1818–25 Showing the "Italian"
pattern. £300–350/$450–525,
with stand £350–450/$525–675

▲ **A saucer in the**
**"Waterloo", or**
**"Italian Church",**
**pattern,** *c.*1820
This is the rarest of the
Italian-influenced
patterns by Spode.
£190–250/$285–375

▶ **A cheese stand by Spode,** *c.*1820
In the "Bridge of Lucano" pattern.
£250–350/$375–525

Porta Salara, Rome. The pattern was very popular with schools, hospitals, and institutions, whose wares often bore their individual crest. Begun in 1815, it continues in production to the present day; in 1860 it was produced by Copeland in a very dark, inky, flow-like blue that proved very popular with the North American market. Many large decorative items suitable for conservatories were produced in this dark colour, such as Ashanti stools and garden seats. Large bathroom wares were also made. The early 1920s saw the growth of pink, which remained popular, and the paler blue was reintroduced around 1960 for the European market.

The "Rome" ("Tiber") pattern, introduced around 1811, is from a Merigot aquatint showing the Bridge and Castel Sant'Angelo in Rome. Trajan's Column, at the right of the picture, does not feature in the original engraving. The border is unusually narrow, leaving more room for the pattern. The clarity of image is among the best of all Spode patterns. Thomas Lakin also made this pat-

tern, though his version is not so crisp, and the border is heavier, with large circles making it more prominent and detracting from the pattern. "Rome" is still produced today – a limited edition cheese cradle made in 2002, will undoubtedly one day be a collectors' item.

The "Bridge of Lucano" pattern is taken from an engraving by George Hackett entitled *The Bridge of Lucano near Tivoli in the east of Rome*. It is dominated by a large tower on a bridge, with cattle in the foreground. The border of flowers, leaves, and ears of corn is quite unique to this design. Swansea is another factory that produced this pattern, and there is a version by an unknown maker with the title printed in blue, on the back framed within a ribbon.

The final pattern is "Italian Church" (or "Waterloo"). This is said to depict the church in the Belgian village of Waterloo, close to Wellington's headquarters in 1815 before the famous battle. It is a fairly rare pattern that seems to appear only tableware – usually cups, saucers, and small plates.

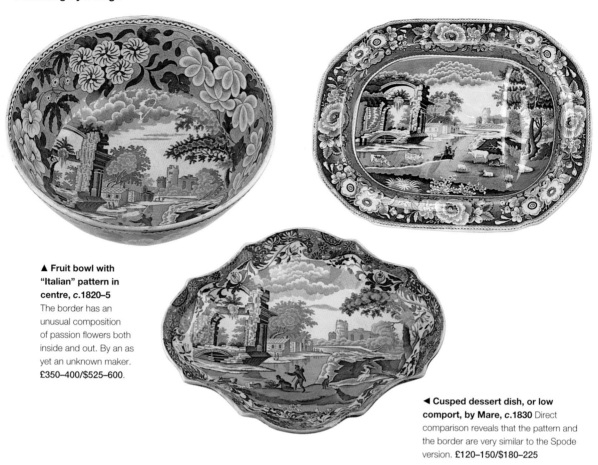

**▲ Fruit bowl with "Italian" pattern in centre, *c.*1820–5** The border has an unusual composition of passion flowers both inside and out. By an as yet an unknown maker. £350–400/$525–600.

**◄ Cusped dessert dish, or low comport, by Mare, *c.*1830** Direct comparison reveals that the pattern and the border are very similar to the Spode version. £120–150/$180–225

# The "Italian" Pattern: Non-Spode

As with any popular design, Spode's "Italian" pattern inspired numerous imitations. Examples are known from factories such as Zachariah Boyle, Edward Challinor, Wood and Challinor, Mare, Pountney & Co., Pountney and Allies, Pountney and Goldney, and, notably, Stubbs.

Most of the variations in pattern are very subtle; some may not even be apparent until examples are placed next to a Spode version. The shade of blue varies, some displaying a greenish tint in certain lights, and the quality of the engraving ranges from acceptable to poor. The number of sheep or figures varies, as well as the plants – especially the large flowers in the foreground. The rock formation to the right or even the building behind the ruined arch of the aqueduct can change subtly.

The individual shapes of dishes, bowls, tureens, and dessert comports help to identify possible manufacturers. This cannot always be relied upon, though, as sometimes a particular potter, faced with a rush order to produce, might have bought in plain undecorated blank shapes from other potters, so adding to the confusion in attribution.

The most obviously different design is the Stubbs version. The border is composed of small dog roses with an outer border of small circles. The cattle are emerging from the water onto the riverbank, with more prominent cattle in the foreground, and the two figures at the water edge are facing away from the water rather than towards it. The figure seated near the tree in the Spode version is missing, the engraving of the buildings is not so sharp, and the joins in the border are more noticeable, as are the smudges on the edge. Having said all this, the Stubbs design is quite uncommon, and in that sense fairly desirable – it can take fifteen years to find a perfect example, as it did with the platter illustrated.

Collecting the non-Spode "Italian" pattern can be exciting, and because examples are few and far

◄ **A rare Stubbs platter with "Circa 1820" impressed on reverse** A border of wild roses, and slight variations to the central "Italian" pattern. "Well-and-tree" style, to allow meat juices to drain.
£550–650/$825–975

▲ **A sauce tureen base made by the Bristol pottery Poutney & Allies, c.1830** Impressed mark. The pattern appears more primitive in design than versions by other manufacturers.
£190–250/$285–375

between the expense is low in comparison to other fields of collecting. Also, the items are not likely to take over your home.

Even though the colour, engraving, and clarity of the design are of lower quality (though the bowl opposite, with the passion flower border, is of equal or possibly greater quality, despite the maker remaining a mystery), these objects have an individual charm of their own. When they are placed together, the variety of colour, shape, and design is more apparent than if you were concentrating on one factory. A good idea would be to include some Spode or Copeland examples to add interest.

# Backstamps for non-Spode "Italian" Designs

◄ **Mare backstamp from comport opposite** Impressed marks are not always easy to make out if they were stamped unevenly.

◄ **Stubbs backstamp from platter oppposite** Stamped marks are made before first firing.

Both the backstamps shown here are of the impressed type: that is, they are stamped into the biscuit before the first firing. They can sometimes be difficult to see as the impression may not have been evenly made, and may be missing one or more letters.

Other impressed marks for this design include "Boyle" for Zachariah Boyle; "Pountney and Allies" forming an almost anchor shape; while Pountney & Co, and Poutney and Goldney just used their respective names in a straight line. At this stage it was usually only the maker's mark that was impressed into the clay, as the final pattern of the object may not have been known.

Printed marks were applied using a transfer at the same time as the decoration, so were always underglaze-printed. Examples of this are Challinor, and Wood and Challinor. The Challinor mark is printed in full, while Wood and Challinor are marked as "W & C", or slightly later as "W. C. & Co.". These marks often include the title of the pattern.

Patterns sometimes appear with the incorrect name on the back, partly because of the poor level of education of the girls working in the factories at the time.

It is likely that other factories also produced versions of this pattern, as many pieces remain unmarked and unatttributed.

**▼ A rare puzzle jug, *c.*1820**
From the "Wild Rose" border series, showing Nuneham Courtenay, near Oxford. Maker unknown.
£2,000–2,500/$3,000–3,750

**▲ A large lidded pot, *c.*1825**
Possibly a slop pail. In the "Wild Rose" border series, showing Nuneham Courtenay, near Oxford. Maker unknown.
£1,500–2,200/$2,250–3,300

# The "Wild Rose" border series

The "Wild Rose" border series takes its name from its very attractive border of dog roses. The pattern was first produced around 1825–1830, and was the first English landscape pattern to be transfer-printed on to pottery. Many different factories made it (including Bell, Bovey Tracey, Clementson, Fell, Meir, Moore, Podmore Walker, Twigg, and Wood) and so the quality of the engraving varies very much, as does the potting – some pieces are very fine, while others are crude.

The design most commonly associated with this series shows a view of Nuneham House, at Nuneham Courtenay, near Abingdon in Oxfordshire. The source print for this design is thought to be an engraving by W.B. Cooke, after a drawing by Samuel Owen published in 1811, showing the house and park, built in 1756 for the first Earl of Harcourt. Capability Brown, the well-known designer, landscaped these famous grounds in the latter part of the eighteenth century. In the picture, Nuneham House is on the left-hand side and a tower on the right; however, the latter is not found in the source print, and is thought to be a neo-Gothic tower that was planned but never built. The main features of the design are two punts in the foreground, (possibly the Stanton Harcourt ferry), the lock keeper's thatched cottage, and the rustic bridge, which originally formed part of the riverside walk as designed by Capability Brown.

The pattern was applied to many different objects, some quite unusual. Some very interesting puzzle jugs seem to appear in this pattern, such as the one above; and the larger, better quality platters look very impressive. You may like to collect this pattern in order to make up a composite dinner service for practical use. Very few examples of the pattern are marked with a potter's name, even though it is known to have been produced by over twenty different factories. Some are even printed with "Improved Wild Rose" in underglaze blue, but the design is just the same.

◄ **A rare garniture vase, c.1820**
Showing the "Village Church"
pattern. Maker unknown.
£550–600/$825–900

▲ **An arcaded plate
from a dessert
service, c.1825**
Showing Nuneham
Courtenay. On
arcaded plates the
border is omitted
from the pattern.
Maker unknown.
£150–190/$225–285

► **Plate by Hamilton, c.1825**
Showing the "Philosopher" pattern.
£90–130/$135–195

As with any pattern produced by many factories, there are some subtle differences in the basic pattern – the number of sheep on the hill or the thatch on the cottage for instance – though these are only usually evident when several items are put together.

Another very similar pattern, which shares an identical border, is the "Village Church" pattern. This pattern shows a typical English rural village scene; a prominent church in the background, fields, a thatched cottage, and two men talking beside an open gate, while the number of sheep in the foreground varies with the maker. No source print has so far been found for this pattern. It is known to have been produced by several factories, but a marked piece has yet to be discovered. It has been known to be marked "Rural Village", but none has been found with a factory mark.

Unlike the "Nuneham Courtenay" pattern, most of this is generally of good quality; the engraving can in fact be very fine, as can the potting. Much less was produced, so not surpris-

ingly fewer perfect pieces have survived. Some very unusual shapes do appear in this pattern, however: it was not confined to tableware. This would be a very good example of an English rural scene to collect, as the prices are not usually as high as other rural designs – it seems to be a greatly underrated pattern.

Another pattern with the "Wild Rose" border is the "Philosopher", made by Hamilton of Stoke-on-Trent around 1820. It shows the "philosopher" standing on a ruin, with a seated companion, talking to two figures in the foreground. The scene is rural in nature – you can make out a church on the hill, as well as a cottage, a bridge, and also a waterfall, with cattle in the foreground. The quality of this pattern is usually good, but it is possible that one other factory may also have produced it, as some examples are not so well potted. The "Philosopher" appears to occur mainly on tableware, in a darker blue than the two previous patterns, and is relatively easy to find.

◄ **A plate from the Adams "Regent's Park" series, c.1820** Showing the "Residence of the Marquis of Hertford". £130–170/$195–255

► **A plate by William Adams, c.1820**
From the "Flowers & Leaves" border series, showing "Gracefield, Ireland". £220–270/$330–405

# Export Wares

English pottery was exported to North America in large quantities from the last quarter of the eighteenth century. The style was considered to be of superior quality, and so was preferred to other European wares. The exports ceased between 1812 and 1815 when England was at war with America, but soon after the peace treaty between the two countries was signed the lucrative export trade from Staffordshire recommenced.

New designs by factories such as Adams, Enoch Wood, and Clews, to name a few, were produced to show American triumphs in battle and historical events. Ridgway produced a series called "Beauties of America" from c.1820, featuring important American buildings and places. Rogers produced the famous pattern of "Boston State House". This series is not often found in the UK. Another Staffordshire potter, Stevenson, produced the "Acorn and Oak Leaf" border series, again showing American locations and monuments of national pride. Stubbs made a very impressive American

historical series with an eagle, scroll, and flower border, which showed scenes such as "Bank of the United States". In 1829 Stubbs sold his business to Thomas Mayer, another Staffordshire potter, who went on to produce the very famous and collectable series entitled "Arms of America". This series shows the coat of arms of the various states in America, and is truly "serial" in that each size of object shows different arms.

Most of the earlier wares for export were produced in a very dark inky blue, the blue covering the entire object with almost no white showing, as was popular with the North American market. The glaze was also very dark, as can be seen on the reverse of an item. Adams and Enoch Wood marked most of their items, unlike others. It is possible that the importers were not keen to have the country of origin known to buyers, which would explain why some factories just marked their wares with a special mark denoting that it was for export only. Some of the importers insisted on

◀ **A plate by Adams,** *c.*1820
Showing "Pier Fishing"
**£190–240/$285–360**

▶ **A plate by Ridgway,** *c.*1825
In the "Beauties of America" series,
showing "City Hall, New York" **£280–340/$420–510**

having their own retailer's mark added to the items, which as may be imagined causes some confusion today. The majority of these marks were printed in underglaze blue.

Clews produced many patterns destined for export, but one of their most famous was the "Dr Syntax" series. The source prints for these were drawings by Thomas Rowlandson, published between 1809 and 1811, illustrating a book by Dr William Combe. The series depicts thirty-two different scenes, some of which are highly amusing, and all identified on the back in underglaze blue. An unknown potter reproduced the series in a more purplish blue during the latter part of the nineteenth century, but the quality of both the engraving and the potting is inferior in this case; also the plates are usually larger in size. The later version is, of course, not marked Clews, and is of less value than the original.

Many British views were produced in the dark export blue, including the "London Views" series

by Enoch Wood, showing various villas in Regent's Park; this series was sourced from Thomas H. Shepherd's *Metropolitan Improvements* drawings, published in 1829. William Adams also produced the "Regent's Park" series from the same source prints. One of the pieces from Enoch Wood's series is an open baking dish showing the "Bank of England", and other views include "Clarence Terrace" and Burton's "Coliseum". All these views are easier to find in America, but are gradually returning to England thanks to the two-way traffic across the Atlantic.

Floral designs were also produced in the dark blue by many factories, particularly Stubbs and Clews: all are very attractive and display great attention to detail.

Potters such as Stevenson and Jackson began to experiment with lighter, more open patterns, showing more white. Most of these used historical subjects, with an extensive production of over forty different views. These included designs by Ralph

**▼ Ewer & bowl by Rogers, c.1815–20**
Showing the "Zebra" pattern.
£750–900/$1,125–1,350

**► A very rare cheese cradle by Clews, c.1820**
In the "Dr Syntax" series, showing "Dr Syntax and
the Gipsies". £4,000–5,000/$6,000–7,500

Stevenson showing Erie Canal, the Shipping Port on the Ohio, New Orleans, and Riceborough, Georgia, all of which formed part of the "Lace Border" series and were also produced in brown, pink, and mauve. The name of the place featured and of the potter are usually marked on the reverse. During the mid-1830s, Jackson produced a variety of wares, notably showing the Baltimore battle monument; Boston State House; Albany, New York; New York City Hall; and Fort Ticonderoca, New York – available in blue, black, brown, green, pink, and mauve. The majority of both these potters' patterns are available only in America, but of course some do appear in England from time to time.

The mid-1830s also saw periods of great industrial unrest in the potteries, with the Chartist movement demanding parliamentary reform; many factories were closed for long periods, and some permanently. The troubles eased in 1837 and the potteries reopened, this time coinciding with a general decline in the demand for blue printed pottery across the Atlantic – caused mainly by America's own financial instability.

After the decline in blue printed exports the importers requested coloured transferware, which was therefore produced in vast quantities – in pink, mulberry, green, brown, and yellow. Some was made using more than one colour, and because it was so popular it superseded the blue. Consequently, coloured transferware is today much more common in America than in Great Britain.

Staffordshire printed pottery was also exported to Canada, though not in such large amounts as to the United States. The "Arctic Scenery" series by an unknown maker, showing various snow scenes, is very popular in Canada, as is the "Polar Bear" found on two patterns: the "Quadrupeds" series by Hall, and the "Sporting" series by Enoch Wood.

Other landscape designs featuring European countries such as France, Italy (many including Naples and Venice), and Germany were produced in large numbers, giving fairly stylized impressions of the lands they depicted. A vast amount of commemorative printed pottery from Staffordshire depicting American heroes was exported; this too was produced in many colours.

◀ **A plate by Ralph Hall, c.1820**
In the "Select Views" series, showing "Pains Hill, Surrey". £225–275/$335–415

▲ **A plate by Godwin, c.1840**
Showing the "William Penn Treaty with the Indians".
£225–275/$335–415

Enoch Wood made the "French" series, c.1818–46, in a very dark blue: of limited appeal, its intended market remains unclear. Views for this series include "Chapelle de Guillaume Tell" (the House of William Tell), "East View of la Grange, the Residence of Marquis Lafayette", and at least fifteen others.

A later production by Anthony Shaw in the 1850s was "The Texian Campaign", another serial pattern said to show various battles of the Mexican War of 1846-48. This pattern is greatly sought after by collectors, but remains scarce outside the United States. The pattern was also made in other colours.

Davenport produced "Views of Montreal" around 1850, showing the *British America*, a paddle-steamer well-known in its time, which plied the river between Quebec and Montreal – the significance of its name is unclear.

There are so many other patterns still to be found, which make this field of collection so exciting and interesting; and of course the limited scope of this book means it is not possible to discuss all the known patterns that are available.

# American Export Marks

▲ **Rare mark from the Rogers ewer & bowl opposite**
An eagle was a typical choice of image for export marks on pottery destined for the United States as it was a well-known national symbol.

Most exporters had a special mark, used on the back of pottery for export only. The mark shown is from the Rogers factory; it is on the underside of a jug and bowl in the "Zebra" pattern. Designs of marks featuring the national symbol of the eagle were prevalent on wares for export to America. The item was not marked as being by Rogers, which is unusual for both the factory and the pattern. As discussed earlier, this may have been because the importer did not wish the buyer to know the country of origin; some items have only the importer's or retailer's stamp.

In 1891 the Ways and Means Committee of the American Congress passed the McKinley Traffic Act, which changed all this. The act stated that all items of foreign manufacture must be stamped with the country of origin. From this date all British pottery had "England" stamped on it. It must be remembered that some factories were doing this at an earlier date, and conversely items that were not for export and were produced later can be found without the "England" stamp. The "Made in England" stamp was introduced in the early years of the twentieth century.

▼ **A garden seat by Copeland, *c*.1850** In a flow blue design.
£900–1,200/$1,350–1,800

▲ **A footbath jug by Swansea in the "Lazuli" pattern, *c*.1840** Note the extra front handle for lifting.
£1,200–1,600/$1,800–2,400

# Flow Blue

Flow blue was first introduced around 1830–40. The name describes the technique of decorating earthenware pottery with a dark blue colour, which is then made to smudge, or "flow", from the original transfer design into the white. This "flowing" is the result of the chemical reaction with a solution of lime or ammonia, which is placed in the oven during the final glaze firing.

This technique, which is also known as "flown", was particularly popular with the North American market. Many of the designs were based on a more stylized "Willow"-type pattern. Many floral patterns were also used – clearly influenced by the Chinese style, with large daisy-like flowers and Oriental trees. The designs usually cover most of the object and can often appear as a large splash of deep blue. Another very popular design was a blue marble effect, which on casual inspection appears very realistic; the "Lazuli" pattern by Swansea is a good example of this, mostly used on toilet wares. Some middle class families used these designs to decorate their homes

as it was of course much cheaper than real marble.

Because most flow blue patterns were produced after the introduction of the Acts of Copyright of 1842, they are usually marked with the maker's name, country of origin, and the pattern name. Some included the diamond registration mark giving the full date of manufacture and even the parcel number; a guide to this can be found in specialist books on ceramic marks (*see* "Further Reading", page 153). England was by far the most prolific producer, but during the second half of the nineteenth century the United States and many European countries produced their own.

Not all flow blue is heavily decorated; some is much subtler, with the colour flowing only slightly from the transfer pattern. This type of design became more popular in the last quarter of the nineteenth century. The lighter, cleaner kind was more desirable for use with floral and art nouveau designs.

Sheet patterns are also found in this style (where the whole item is covered using a wallpaper-type

▶ **A round three-part soap dish, *c*.1880** In a flow blue pattern. £60–80/$90–120

▼ **Two bud vases, *c*.1860** Decorated in flow blue, one with overglaze decoration of red and gold. **£60–90/$90–135 each**

▲ **An unusual dog bowl, *c*.1840** Printed in a flow blue pattern. **£1,200–1,500/$1,800–2,250**

transfer). Gilding was often added to the rim of the finished item, creating a less weighty appearance. Embellishments in other colours were applied using bright enamels, either under the glaze before the final firing, giving a permanent finish, or on top of the glaze, making it liable to chip and wear from use. It is very important to check items such as these for signs of wear, as it can greatly affect their value.

The heavily decorated patterns restore very well so take care when buying to check for signs of any restoration – look in particular at vulnerable areas such as handles, spouts, and rims. Run a finger lightly over these parts to determine any change in texture, as repairs often feel slightly rougher than the rest of the pottery; also, there may be a difference in the temperature over the area. Experience will help to perfect your skill in spotting restoration.

Because of the vast amount of flow blue that was manufactured and the fact that it was not so popular in England, examples can be found more cheaply than the traditional printed pottery. That said, larger

and more decorative items such as vases, garden seats, footbaths, and jugs hold their prices well. One important thing to consider when starting a collection of flow blue is the strength of the colour, which can be overpowering and does not blend in very well with other types of blue-and-white pottery, though in the right setting it can be very decorative.

There is a great deal of brand new reproduction china imported from the Far East that is made to resemble flow blue. At a distance it can be difficult to spot – the glaze is a very dark, inky blue covering the item both inside and out, often with runs and bubbles in it. The colour is brighter and harder, and the pattern has no depth or shading. A very indistinct mark is applied to the underside. The general feel to the item is quite different from the genuine article, and if the item is damaged you can see that the underlying pottery is of a chalky, coarse appearance. There is nothing wrong with buying a modern reproduction, providing it is sold as such and does not claim to be an antique.

▼ **An umbrella, or stick, stand by Cauldon,** *c.*1890
In a landscape pattern. Note how the design is joined
to fill the large area to be decorated.
£1,100–1,500/$1,650–2,250

# Later patterns

Many of the blue printed patterns continued to be produced well into the twentieth century, and even into the twenty-first – notably at the Spode factory, which became Copeland around 1850. They continued many designs, especially the Italian-influenced patterns such as the "Italian" and the "Tower". The later "Tower" pattern was produced on many large and very decorative items for the conservatory, garden, and hall, such as garden seats, ceramic stools, umbrella stands, lily pans, and jardinières. Although these were produced in large numbers, few perfect examples survive owing to their size, which makes them vulnerable to damage. Many of these were also exported to America, and today they are very sought after in Germany.

Later patterns include polychromatic items, as well as those that were produced during the "Romantic" period of design, after 1830. These designs were much more open, with larger space between the central design and the border.

Though exotic, the pattern names, such as "Medina", "Morea", "Indian Temples", or "Madras", bore no relation to the scenes depicted, and the imagery was much less topographical. These patterns were more mass-produced, leading to less attention to detail and less precise transfer-joining, especially in the borders; the blue is often paler and the white not so crisp. The plates, whose edges may be moulded or gadrooned with a more rococo style, are usually fractionally larger than the earlier patterns. These patterns may therefore be less expensive, but highly decorative.

Minton produced some very attractive designs such as the "Chinese Marine" series of 1835–40, the tureens and shaped dishes of which are interesting; the pattern was also produced for a long period, so pieces are relatively easy to find. A matched complete dinner service is not an impossible goal, though the blues may vary slightly. Another later Minton pattern, produced into the early twentieth century, is the "Genevese", which was used mainly

◄ **A very rare water lily
pan on a square plinth
by Copeland, c.1890**
In the "Tower" pattern; used
in a conservatory to grow
water lilies. £2,000–3,000/
$3,000–4,500

► **A "Rome" cheese cradle by Spode**
Modern reproduction, limited edition from
the "Signature Collection". Marked on
underside as being reproduction.
£100/$150

◄ **A "Italian" pattern dog bowl by Spode**
Also from the limited edition "Signature Collection"
range and marked as a modern reproduction
(2000).**£25/$40**

on toilet wares, although other flatware items can be found. The "Genevese" pattern was used on many different sizes of ewers and basins, so one can usually be found to fit any size of washstand. The various soap dishes and brush vases were made to fit the small holes in the washstand.

The "Abbey" pattern produced by George Jones in the early part of the twentieth century is very popular in all parts of the world. It is marked "Abbey 1790" (the date the pattern was first registered rather than the date of the item), is quite dark blue in colour, and usually of good quality. The most famous objects produced in the pattern are the Shredded Wheat dishes, which came in two sizes, which were acquired by collecting tokens from cereal boxes in the 1930s. They were reintroduced recently for a short time, and one day are likely to become collectors' items. The design was obviously the pattern of choice for token collectors: a tea set could also be bought using coupons saved from cigarette packets.

The "Asiatic Pheasant" pattern produced by many potters never seems to lose its popularity. It shows several pheasants and large flowers in the centre, within a floral border, although the blue is sometimes so pale that it is difficult to make out the design. It is also available in grey, pink, green, and possibly brown. Many people buy this range for practical use; in the 1990s it was reintroduced by Habitat and featured in many cookery books. Only the basic dinner service was available new, so collectors started to supplement their modern service with more unusual items such as sauce tureens, cheese stands, salt cellars, and pepper pots for everyday use.

The modern items produced by Spode in their limited edition range are also worthy of mention being exact copies of the originals and made with the same techniques. They are all clearly marked on the underside as reproductions, which avoids any question of deception; they are sure to become very collectable in the future.

# Collecting by Decoration

## Decorative motifs and subjects combine to provide endless opportunity

## "Crown, Acorn, & Oak Leaf" border series

John Meir made the "Crown, Acorn, & Oak Leaf" border series in the Tunstall area of Staffordshire, where the factory was in production from 1812 to 1836. Most of the items from this series were probably made in the period after 1820. The pattern takes its name from the border of oak leaves and acorns, and the crown on the backstamp, above the name of the place illustrated. Ralph Stevenson produced a similar series, with fewer acorns in the border and without the crown in the backstamp.

The pattern is a true "serial" pattern, in that each size of plate has a different central picture while all share the same border. The soup tureen (it seems that most of the items in this series are tableware, though that does not mean that other items do not exist) has one picture on the lid, another on the inside, another on the side, and a final one on the undertray. It was often thought that the items did not match, but they were meant to be this way.

Various British country views are depicted, mostly country houses, all in a rather a dull medium blue without a high sheen to the glaze. Not all examples are marked with the name of the place pictured, so it can be fun researching in books and on the Internet to find the original engraving. The series is known to contain twenty-two named views, but there may be more, as both collectors and dealers find new ones from time to time. It is possible that all the engravings derive from the same source, though further research is needed on this subject. Many topographical subjects were taken from J. Preston Neale's book of engravings entitled *Views of the Seats of Noblemen and Gentlemen in England, Scotland, Wales, and Ireland*.

Many areas of the British Isles are depicted in this series, though occasionally you do find different shapes sharing the same engraving – the scene of Balborough Hall in Derbyshire, on the dessert comport shown above, has also been found on a soup plate. Because dessert services were not produced in such great quantities as normal dinner services, a separate copper plate was not produced.

▶ A "Crown, Acorn, & Oak Leaf" dessert comport by Meir, *c.*1825 Showing "Balborough Hall, Derbyshire".
£250–290/$375–435

▼ A spoon rest from the same series, by Meir, *c.*1825 Showing "Worsted House".
£190–250/$285–375

▲ Another Meir plate from the same series, *c.*1825 Showing "Lampton Hall, Durham".
£220–260/$330–390

The shape of the comport is ideal for being displayed flat on the top of a dresser or a table. In fact its distinctive form helped to confirm that John Meir was indeed the maker of this series. Unlike other serial patterns there appears to be more than one picture used for plates and soup plates.

The pickle dish, or spoon rest, is an unusual shape (so it could be used for either purpose) and is unmarked. The source print of Worsted House was found in J. Preston Neale's book of engravings – after much searching of the eleven-volume work! The collecting of source prints to match the pottery provides another interesting aspect to collecting.

Small nursery plates are often the only size that will fit onto the bottom shelf of a dresser. It is a good idea to buy every one you see, as they are more difficult to find than the larger plates – as with all small items, more were lost and broken; also the original service would comprise at least twenty-four dinner plates, but only twelve of the smaller sizes. Small plates can be very stained, as they are often used as butter dishes or ashtrays. Never attempt to try to clean these using household bleach, as this will damage the glaze and may discolour the item. Cleaning of antique pottery should always be left to the professional dealer or ceramic restorer.

A collection of this series can be a source of particular enjoyment to the owner, evoking memories of places visited; and as each individual size of item has a different central design, the interest is enhanced by variety, despite being a single series. The platters or meat dishes are particularly impressive, ranging in size from 30cm (12in) to 53cm (21in), providing a good centrepiece for a dresser or wall display.

Although this series cannot be described as rare, it is unlikely that it was made in vast quantities, and it can be fairly difficult to find. However, occasionally whole groups may become available at once – the market is very dependent on the sale of whole collections and estates: an unpredictable factor that only adds more excitement to collecting.

# The "Bluebell" & "Foliage" border series

The two factories William Adams, and James and Ralph (J. & R.) Clews, produced the "Bluebell" border series, whose name derives from the drooping blubells amongst other flowers in the border. In both cases the borders are identical, but the only known view shared by both potters is of St Mary's Abbey, York. The two examples used here are both by Clews. As can be seen from the illustrations, they were made in two shades of blue; the paler version for the English home market and the darker for the American export market.

It is thought that the source for the engraving for some of this series is once again John Preston Neale. The soup tureen shown here depicts two views of Fonthill Abbey near Salisbury, Wiltshire, built by William Thomas Beckworth in the late eighteenth and early nineteenth century, after inheriting the Fonthill estate from his father together with a sizeable fortune. The tower was built in such a way – too large, and without adequate foundations – that it collapsed in 1825,

destroying much of the abbey. Views of Fonthill are difficult to find, as there is a very active Beckworth society whose members seem to find them all!

The soup plate illustrated showing Tintern Abbey, Monmouthshire, originally the home of the Lord of Chepstow, is printed in the paler, arguably more attractive blue, showing the print to its best advantage. You may be able to spot an imperfection on the inner rim of the soup plate: this is caused by shrinkage of the biscuit clay during the initial firing. Although not damage as such, it does affect the value of the plate. Having said this, the series is quite rare, and so not the cheapest. It is another serial pattern comprising many views – there are at least twenty-three by Adams and eighteen by Clews. Both factories' versions and shades of blue mix and match very well together; a complete service in either pattern would be an impressive sight.

The "Foliage" border is yet another serial pattern, produced by three factories, William

◀ **A soup plate in the "Foliage" border series, *c.*1820** Maker so far unknown. Showing a view of Windsor Castle, across the River Thames. £200–250/$300–375

▶ **A 20cm (8in) dessert plate in the "Foliage" border series, *c.*1820** Showing Gunton Hall, Norfolk. Maker unknown. £120–160/$180–240

Adams, J. & R. Clews, and an unknown maker. The Adams and Clews versions are both marked with the maker's name and the outer border has a narrow strip of scrolls. The unknown maker's version was most likely made exclusively for the North American market, as it is printed in a very dark inky blue: the almost total absence of white makes the scene somewhat indistinct in some cases. The lack of a maker's mark may be because most of it was exported and, as we have seen, it was common for the importer not to want his clients to know the country of origin.

The view of Gunton Hall, Norfolk (shown on the dessert plate above) is probably one that turns up most frequently in Britain. Gunton Hall is still in use as a holiday centre today, and is now in the county of Suffolk. The soup plate shows a view of Windsor Castle from the Eton side of the River Thames; similar views of of this scene were popular with other potters. Most of the places featured seem to be from England alone – famous

places, including Blenheim Palace, Oxfordshire, of Badminton Horse trial fame; another view of Fonthill Abbey; Gorhambury, Hertfordshire; and other views in Buckinghamshire, Cornwall, and Yorkshire, to name only a few.

These very dark items are difficult to display, and they benefit from the use of spotlights in order to avoid the effect of a mass of very dull, dark blue. Great care should be taken when purchasing pottery printed in such a dark blue – scratches and knife marks are so much more visible. If the piece is dirty, blemishes may be hidden to begin with – you may wash items of this nature only to find they look much worse when clean, as the white of the pottery showing through cannot be disguised. The glaze of dark items seems to damage more easily, giving a very dull appearance. Also, beware of restorations, as they do not show so much on this colour. This is one series for which it is particularly important to look carefully for wares in perfect condition.

**▼ A platter in the "Tulip" border series,** *c.*1820–5 Maker unknown. Showing "A View of Green Park" and Westminster Abbey, London. £1,000–1,400/$1,500–2,100

**▲ A platter in the "Pineapple" border series showing Barnard Castle in Durham, *c.*1820–5** An impressive example at 48cm (19in) in width; it was only made in this size, so only one platter was produced per dinner service. The maker of this series is unknown at present. £900–1,200/$1,350–1,800

# The "Tulip" & "Pineapple" border series

The "Tulip" border series takes its name, as might be imagined, from the very wide border containing tulips. The series is not commonly found. Most of the engravings are taken from John Britton and Edward Brayley's *Beauties of England and Wales*, published in London between 1801 and 1808 in twenty-six volumes. The maker of the pottery is unknown, though its date of manufacture is around 1825–30, and the quality of both the transferring and the potting is generally very good. One of the most common designs in the series is of St Albans Abbey in Hertfordshire, which appears on soup and dinner plates. Several other potters also produced scenes of St Albans Abbey, although each shows a different view. St Albans was a very important town, where England's first Christian martyr died in the third century.

The border extends inwards much further than is usual with other patterns, providing a very attractive frame to the central picture. The platters are oval in shape and come in three known designs,

including the two illustrated here. The larger is "A View of Green Park" with Westminster Abbey in the background, the source print for which is from *Ackerman's Repository of Fine Arts*; the smaller is "Bridge and Castle at Brecknock, South Wales", from an engraving published in London in 1813 by J. Harris, of St Paul's Church Yard. The third is recorded as "Alexandra Pope's Villa on the Thames at Twickenham", and in size is in between the two illustrated.

A part dinner service exists in this pattern (that the author is yet to see), which may give further clues as to the possible manufacturer, as there should be some tureens in it. Tureens and shaped dishes always help in the identification of a manufacturer, as the shape, handle, or finials are often particular to one or two potters. The colour of the series strengthens the likelihood that it was made for the English market. This particular pattern would be great fun to collect, involving as it would researching the various source prints, and perhaps

**► A smaller platter in the "Tulip" border series, c.1820–5**
A bridge and ruined castle believed to be "Bridge and Castle at Brecknock, South Wales". Platters in this series are not common.
£600–750/$900–1,125

**▼ A 20cm (8in) cheese or dessert plate from the "Pineapple" border series, c.1820**
Showing Dalberton Tower, Wales, at the "gateway to Snowdonia."
£160–190/$240–285

**◄ A dinner plate in the "Pineapple" border series, c.1820** Showing a view of St Albans Abbey, Hertfordshire. The same view is also included in the "Antique Scenery" series on a small platter.
£140–190/$210–285

eventually even finding the identity of the maker.

The "Pineapple" border series is not as varied as other patterns, depicting mainly ruined castles and abbeys. The maker is not known, but there is some debate as to the possibility of it being John Meir, though this is yet to be proved conclusively. It was made around 1820–5, and the quality of both the printing and the glaze varies greatly – there seems to have been a lack of quality control on the part of the factory, and the plates are heavy and usually of lesser quality than the larger items. The border consists of large flowers and scrolls, and small inverted pineapples. The name of the place depicted is printed on the reverse in a very decorative scroll surrounded by flowers, but beware: it is not always correct. The plate shown here of St Albans Abbey was marked as being Knaresborough Abbey, in Yorkshire. Mistakes such as this may have been caused by the lack of education of the girls who were employed as transferrers at the time.

There are some collectors who only collect items from a particular part of the country, so if Yorkshire is your forte this is a good series – it appears to show mostly views of Yorkshire, along with a few in Wales and the west of England. The significance of this is not known. The source for the design was *The Antiquities of Great Britain*, reproduced in *Views of Monasteries, Castles, and Churches* engraved by W. Byrne from drawings by Thomas Hearne, published in 1807.

The series is not rare, as so much was produced, but items of good quality can be hard to find. The platters are very impressive (especially the larger ones) but, as with most picture plates, they are not cheap. A good relationship with a specialist is a great help in finding quality items from this series, which is all the more desirable because the mellowness of blue means that it will blend in with other patterns without overwhelming the rest of a collection. It is always worth considering how new pieces will fit in with the rest of your collection.

▼ **A plate by Enoch Wood, c.1820** From the "Grapevine" border series, showing Guys Cliff, Warwickshire. £240–275/$360–415

◄ **A plate by Belle Vue Pottery, Yorkshire, c.1830** Showing Durham Cathedral. "Belle Vue" is an uncommon series. £170–220/$255–330

▼ **A platter by Enoch Wood, c.1820** From the "Grapevine" border series, showing Windsor Castle from the River Thames. £1,000–1,300/$1,500–1,950

# The "Grapevine" border series & other serial patterns

Enoch Wood of Burslem, Staffordshire, often described as the father of the potteries, produced the "Grapevine" border series around 1820–5. This is the most extensive of all serial designs, containing over sixty-five different patterns. The series is characterized by its border of vines, leaves, and grapes, and most of the items are marked with the maker's name and the title of the place pictured. The colour is fairly dark in colour and was popular for the export market, which may explain why some items were not marked. Many examples have been found in the United States and found their way back to England.

John Preston Neale's *Views of the Seats of Noblemen and Gentlemen in England and Wales, Scotland and Ireland* appears to be the source for the design, providing some very interesting scenes, as well as shapes, to be collected. However, some of the pictures are identical to ones found in other series because they share the same source print. The quality of both the printing and glazing is usually very good. Some of the blue is even darker, which may be because it was made at a different time: in the early nineteenth century, without today's computer mixing of colour, it was impossible to achieve an exact match.

Tableware items are the most commonly found pieces, but of course this is not to say that other objects with the pattern were not produced. Examples of plates and soup plates are found quite easily, but platters, small cheese and side plates, and other shapes are more elusive as there were fewer of them in the original dinner service. The plates and soup plates, unlike in most other series, are available in several designs, as are the tureens and bases. As with some other serial patterns, tureens are composed of up to four different patterns on the separate parts, including the lid, base, and ladle.

The series by Belle Vue pottery is quite an uncommon one, the author having found some pieces only after much searching. Established in 1802 through a partnership involving Job and

**◄ A soup plate from the Belle Vue pottery, c.1825** From the "Belle Vue" series, showing Guys Cliff, Warwickshire. £170–220/$255–330

**▼ A small plate from the "Antique Scenery" series, c.1825** Showing Wingfield Castle. The back of the plate is incorrectly marked Fonthill Abbey. £70–130/$105–195

**▼ A platter from the "Antique Scenery" series, c.1825** Showing "North East View of Lancaster". £650–750/$975–1,125

George Ridgway, the pottery operated from Hull, Yorkshire, and was taken over by William Bell in 1826, closing finally in 1841. So far around ten views have been found, and of course there may be more. The central designs are almost identical to those used by other potters on earlier wares, their source being J.S. Storer and J. Greig's *The Antiquarian and Topographical Cabinet*, published between 1807 and 1811, with most of the scenes seeming to be from the northern half of the British Isles. The colour is a pale to medium blue with an attractive border, and the title of the pattern is usually printed on the reverse. Examples are also known to have been produced in other colours. The quality of the pieces is generally very good, the print being clear and the glaze having a high gloss to it, so pieces are quickly sold once put on display.

The "Antique Scenery" series is an interesting one, produced in 1825–30 by an as yet an unknown maker. The source for the design is Byrne's *Antiquities of Great Britain*, with the pattern printed in a pale to medium blue, sometimes almost grey in colour. It is very extensive, with many variations appearing on the plates. The name of the view is printed on the reverse in a cartouche, below a crown. Again, beware of mistakes – the small nursery plate illustrated is marked "Fonthill Abbey" when in fact it shows Wingfield Castle, Suffolk.

The backs of the larger plates in this series are often combed (that is, they have ridges runing along the base), presumably to provide grip and so stop them slipping when in use. The shapes of the dessert service items are distinctive, yet we do not seem any nearer to discovering the maker. In fact, the quality of the colour and the transfer varies so much that there may have been more than one maker. The cost is usually less than for some of the other pictorial series, but the price for meat plates appears to be rising – especially for the larger ones. This is a very collectable series, which again mainly seems to be available only on tableware.

▶ A platter by Thomas & Benjamin
Godwin, c.1809–34
A "View of London", with St Paul's
Cathedral on the left and the Shot
Tower on the right. The smoke on the
bridge is coming from the Shot Tower
works on the bank of the Thames.
£900–1,400/$1,350–2,100

# Cities & Towers: London

There have been probably more views produced of London using the transfer printing process than of anywhere else. The "Villa in Regent's Park" series by Enoch Wood shows two views printed in very dark blue, which were both taken from Shepherd's *Metropolitan Improvements*. William Adams produced three different views in his "Regent's Park" series, using these same source prints. William Ridgway made the "Osterley Park" pattern, showing an arched bridge in a very rural landscape – now the site of the M4 motorway, as is the view near Colnebrook.

Ralph Hall produced another series in dark blue called "Picturesque Scenery", which includes a view of Fulham Church. Carey, in the famous "Cathedral" series, offers a wonderful view of St Paul's Cathedral on the largest platter and drainer. Goodwins and Harris made the "Metropolitan Scenery" series showing more than sixteen views of London and the surrounding area, going out as far as Windsor and Eton. The scene illustrated here is the "View of Woolwich", which although known to exist has not been illustrated before. The border to the series has a profusion of passion flowers – not to be confused with the "Passion Flower" border series, which is of a paler shade of blue. Other views in the "Metropolitan Scenery" series include Bow Bridge, North End Hampstead, Greenwich, Blackheath, Waltham Cross, and Twickenham.

The single pattern piece illustrated here, showing a "View of London", was made by Thomas and Benjamin Godwin around 1825–30 at the Canal Works, Burslem, Staffordshire. The picture shows a panoramic view of the London skyline, with St Paul's Cathedral in the background and the old London Bridge with the Shot Tower on the right. The pattern is the same on each item, but the smaller items do not include the Shot Tower, and it appears to have been produced only on dinnerware. The pattern amply makes up for the plainness of the tureens; in fact the larger platters are very striking.

Enoch Wood used more than twenty scenes for

his "London Views" series, printed in dark blue. Most of them were intended for the American export market – the open baking dish depicting the Bank of England, illustrated here, was purchased in America. Other views in the series include Clarence Terrace, the Coliseum, Cumberland Terrace, Finsbury Chapel, and Limehouse Dock, among many others. This series has a very similar border to the "Grapevine" border series, except that it is much wider, making a square frame around the central picture and extending quite far into the well of the plate. All the scenes were also taken from Shepherd's *Metropolitan Improvements*.

Another scene favoured by several factories depicts Richmond Bridge spanning the River Thames. The one illustrated is by William Mason, made around 1825 for the "Beaded Frame" series – named after the oblong frame of beads on the reverse of the items, in which the title of the scene is printed. Though this is an extensive series, Richmond appears to be its only London view.

The border of the platter illustrated is "clobbered", meaning that the flowers are hand-painted in enamel after the final firing of the glaze. As with all clobbered items, care should be taken to ensure that the enamel is not chipped or rubbed. The border area is very susceptible to damage, especially if the plates are stacked during storage. Pay particular attention to any areas where the enamel may have been touched up. Close inspection often reveals that any new paint is not as thick as the original. The series is available without any embellishment, though more often the outer rim is painted in a dark crimson, or sometimes gilded.

Other views of Richmond Bridge were produced by Enoch Wood in the "Grapevine" border series, by Poutney and Allies in the "River Thames" series, by Elkin and Knight in the "Rock Cartouche" series, and by Harvey in the "Towns and Cities" series. All the factories appear to have used the same source print, and all show the bridge rather than the town.

▶ **A water jug by the
Bristol pottery
Poutney & Allies,
c.1816–35**
A "View of Bristol
Harbour".
£500–600/$750–900

▲ **A 20cm (8in) plate
by John & William
Ridgway, c.1825**
From the "College
Views" series, showing
Clare College,
Cambridge.
£180–220/$270–330

▲ **A toilet box by Poutney & Allies,
c.1816–35**
View of Bristol Harbour.
£300–350/$450–525

# Other Cities & Towns

A very famous series, produced around 1825–30 by John and William Ridgway and entitled "College Views", features most of the Oxbridge colleges. The potting of this series is of excellent quality – the author has yet to find a poor example. Each college featured is framed in an octagonal white frame, with a border of flowers and medallions showing cherubs and a goat. The series is printed in a dark to medium "Oxford blue" – even the Cambridge colleges.

There are two views of Christ Church, Oxford; otherwise, each college is depicted only once, sometimes only on lids or tureen bases. Many alumni attempt to find a plate featuring their own college – though the ones that are featured on large platters may well be beyond the financial reach of most students or new graduates. The plates are usually fairly easy to obtain, the dinner and soup plates being the easiest, again because more were included in the original dinner services. The pattern seems to appear only on dinner and dessert services, including pickle dishes, chestnut baskets, stands, and knife rests. There is also be a wine cooler in the series. The view illustrated is of Clare Hall, Cambridge, also showing the River Cam. Other factories, such as Enoch Wood and Harvey, made more general views of Oxford and Cambridge.

An unknown maker around 1830 produced a small series featuring Leighton Buzzard in Bedfordshire. The series appears to have been commissioned by the ironmonger, china, glass, and general retailer N. Neale, who had a shop in the market place at Leighton Buzzard. Some of the items include the name Neale on the front – possibly for advertising purposes – but most have it on the reverse. The most common view is of "Leighton Bussard Cross" (note the old spelling of Buzzard), in addition to a view of the church. The border is of blue dog roses and is rather similar to the "Wild Rose" border series.

The quality of the potting varies, none being

◀ **A pouring dessert comport dish, *c*.1830**
Maker unknown; showing Leighton Buzzard Cross,
Bedfordshire (spelt "Bussard" originally). The reverse
is marked N. Neale, the name of an ironmonger in
Leighton Buzzard at the time. **£170–230/$255–345**

▶ **A very rare pitcher
and bowl for a
washstand by
Harvey, *c*.1830**
From the "Cities and
Towns" series, the jug
showing Lancaster and
the bowl Oxford.
**£800–900/$1,200–1,350**

exceptional – though the smaller plates without a
border appear to be of better quality. Leighton
Buzzard being only a small market town, examples
are not common as not so many were made. The
item illustrated is from a dessert service.

Pountney and Allies, a Bristol potter in
production in the early part of the nineteenth
century with several partnerships, depicted an
extensive variety of Bristol views, including the two
illustrated here of the harbour. The series includes
scenes of Bristol Hot Wells (on a platter), Clifton,
Clifton Rocks and St Vincent's Rock, Cooks Folly,
a "View Near Bristol", the River Avon, and
Chepstow Castle, to name only a few.

Most of the places are identified on the reverse
with the name of the place featured. The series is
very sought after by collectors and so usually
commands a high price, even though the quality of
the potting varies. The pattern appears on both
tableware and toilet items, the two pieces illustrated
here being from a toilet set. The jug would

originally have had a bowl to go with it and the
lidded toilet box was used for brushes or razors
on a washstand.

Harvey, in his "Cities" series, featured many
places, including Oxford and Cambridge,
Canterbury, Dublin, Edinburgh, Gloucester,
Greenwich, and others; the view of Greenwich on
a plate is most common, though the series itself is
quite rare. The border to this series is very
distinctive, showing auriculas and leaves within a
scroll, and the whole effect, printed in a medium
blue with the centre of the flowers and the scroll
in a darker blue is most attractive. The example
illustrated is a jug and bowl from a toilet set. The
bowl with the scene of the Oxford skyline and the
river in the foreground is marked "Oxford", while
the jug is unmarked and shows a "North East
View of Lancaster". Another of the many places
featured on blue-and-white pottery is Pultney
Bridge, Bath, produced by Swansea in around
1820 and very collectable.

◀ **A very rare jug, c.1820**
Commemorating the Battle of the Boyne
and William of Orange; maker unkown.
£2,000–2,500/$3,000–3,750

▶ **A platter from the "British History"
series by Jones, c.1826–8**
Showing the "Battle of Waterloo".
£2,500–3,000/$3,750–4,500

# Historical Subjects

Historical subjects are very well covered by blue printed pottery. The most famous example depicting British topics is the "British History" series made by Jones of Hanley in Staffordshire. The factory was only in production for a two-year period, from 1826 to 1828. Very few other examples of Jones's work appear on the market, so it seems feasible that the "British History" series was their main output. The series comprises fifteen to twenty views of notable events from Britain's past.

The pattern has an interesting border of arms, armour, and other military items, alternating with a group of union wreath flowers – the rose, thistle, and shamrock – surrounding a crown and bishop's mitre. It seems that the quality of all the pieces tends to be very high – both in the printing and in the glaze. This is another uncommon series, the plates, as usual, being easier to source than the larger items. Each scene's title is printed on the reverse, with the maker's name on a shield; scenes include the "Battle of Waterloo", the "Coronation of George IV",

"Hamden Mortally Wounded", the "Seven Bishops to the Tower", "Elizabeth Addressing the Troops", and "The Death of Lord Nelson". The two most commonly found views, both depicted on plates, are the "Signing of the Magna Carta" and the "Landing of William of Orange".

Many American historical views also appear on blue printed pottery. Most of these are printed in the dark blue favoured by the American market. John and William Ridgway produced the "Beauties of America" series showing a large selection of buildings of American historical interest, including Boston State House – a view also depicted by Rogers; a view of City Hall, New York; and one of the New York Alms Houses. The "Medallion Portrait" series by Stevenson commemorates various sites of historic interest in America. A series by Anthony Shaw entitled the "Texian Campaign" shows scenes from the American war with Mexico of 1846–8. Examples of this series are not often found in Britain.

◄ **An ale mug printed in puce, *c.*1840**
Showing scenes from the Crimean War;
maker unknown. **£200–250/$300–375**

► **A soup tureen stand from the "British
History" series by Jones, *c.*1826–8**
Showing "The Seven Bishops
going to the Tower".
**£550–750/$825–1,125**

The "William Penn Treaty" series, printed in a pale blue, green, or brown by Thomas Godwin around 1835, shows several views of William Penn making a treaty with the Native American Indians. This is also an uncommon series, with several usually turning up at the same time, probably when a collection is dispersed. A series produced by Charles J. Mason in the late 1830s, called "The Napoleon", depicts the French leader's various battles and achievements. This series was also printed in green and brown, in addition to blue. Another interesting series to collect is one by an unkown maker, usually found on smaller nursery size plates, featuring Father Matthew advocating temperance and lecturing on the evils of alcohol; it appears more usually in black, with varying verses and mottoes.

Vast quantities of jugs, mugs, and plates were produced to commemorate the births, deaths, and coronations of successive kings and queens of England. Some are very finely potted and decorated, usually having a portrait on either side

with the date of the event and the union wreath emblem. A collection devoted exclusively to this subject is very inspiring but also expensive.

The Crimean War and its battles feature strongly on printed pottery. Many examples are found in blue or purple, some with dates and the name of the battle pictured. The quality of these seem to vary – some are very poorly potted and were possibly made as rather cheap mementoes. Other subjects, such as the 1832 Reform Bill, the repeal of the Corn Laws, and railway history, also figure on blue-and-white pottery. Collectors particularly prize railway items. Many items commemorate King Richard III, and William of Orange at the Battle of the Boyne. Most of these are of very good quality, with few appearing in blue: those that do are very sought after. Arguably, some topographical patterns could also be termed historical, as many buildings featured on pottery no longer exist and have therefore become part of history – such as Godwin's Shot Tower in his "View of London".

◄ **A plate by John & Richard Riley, *c.*1825**
Showing an "Eastern Street Scene", a combination of
two Daniell prints: *The Sacred Tree of the Hindoos At
Gyan, Bahar & View on the Chitpore Road, Calcutta.*
**£90–135/$135–205**

► **A platter by William Walsh, *c.*1820**
"View in Fort Madura & the Emperor's Friday
Procession to Prayers". This platter is
exceptionally large – 63.5cm (25in) in width.
**£1,500–2,000/$2,250–3,000**

# The Orient

After the long period dominated by pottery decorated in the Chinese manner, the buying public demanded a wider choice of design. Foreign travel among the middle and upper classes fostered new ideas, and encouraged demands that their experiences be represented on pottery. As we have seen, the publication of various books of engravings of views of Egypt and and other Near- and Middle-Eastern ("Orient" indicated the "East") lands by Luigi Mayer was to provide the inspiration for Spode's "Caramanian" series, introduced in 1810.

This series depicts over twenty views of the south-west region of Turkey, then known as Caramania. As with most of the Spode patterns, the quality is excellent; the placing of the transfers was so accurate that they were always central to the object. The initial cost of production must have been quite high owing to the intricate nature of the engravings. Trees and animals combine to create an interesting border quite unrelated to the rest of the pattern. The central design varies with the shape of the piece to be decorated, reminding us that this is another serial pattern. This design was popular with the buying public – especially when the shapes of the items changed, becoming larger and able to hold more food – and remains so today with collectors.

Another Spode pattern is the "Indian Sporting" series, which shares the same border as the "Caramanian" series. The source for this was Howitt and Williamson's *Oriental Field Sports*, a series of sketches showing various hunting scenes in the Indian jungle and surrounding area. Some of the designs are gruesome, but are nevertheless highly sought after by collectors. An unknown maker made a similar series using a different border, but only three views are known at present. It is in an unusual oval shape, but the printing is fine. Edward Challinor produced a copy of Spode's "Indian Sporting" series and called it "Oriental Sports". Of course the quality is not as high as that of the Spode version, and it was not produced in such numbers.

▲ **A plate by Godwin, from the "Indian Views" series. *c*.1835**
Showing "Sueseya Ghaut Khanpor". £120–190/$180–285

▲ **A platter by Rogers, *c*.1820**
Showing the "Monopteros" pattern.
£600–750/$900–1,125

◄ **A plate by Ridgway, *c*.1820**
From the "Ottoman Empire" series, showing Tchiurluk. Source: Luigi Mayer's *Interesting Views in Turkey.*
£190–240/$285–360

Wedgwood produced only one pattern with an Eastern influence, entitled "Absalom's Pillar", the source for which remains unknown.

Thomas and William Daniell produced six volumes of aquatints entitled *Oriental Scenery*, showing scenes of northern India recorded during their travels. These prints were the basis for many designs used on pottery. Rogers used them on the "Monopteros", the "Camel", and the "Musketeer" patterns. Herculaneum, the Liverpool potter, made an impressive "India" series, showing palaces, tombs, and other glamorous buildings holding great fascination for British consumers. Some feature a procession of people and exotic animals. An unknown potter produced very similar designs to Herculaneum.

Unlike Spode, most of whose patterns derive from one source only, the pattern shown here by John and Richard Riley is a good example of the use of more than one aquatint as the source for the design. In this case two are used – the tree on the left

is from the *Sacred Tree of the Hindoos at Gyan, Bahar*, and the buildings on the right are from *View on the Chitpore Road, Calcutta*, both by Thomas Daniell. The pattern features only one design, which is printed on every item.

Thomas Godwin produced a series entitled "Indian Views" in a paler blue, with the titles of the different scenes printed on the reverse. The ource for all the prints is not known – it would be interesting to research this and then perhaps collect the corresponding engravings or prints.

Another (yet not the final – the reader will find that many more Eastern views were produced in addition to those this book is able to illustrate) extensive series is the "Ottoman Empire" made by John and William Ridgway around 1820, which appears only to have been produced on tableware. The source for this series is again Luigi Mayer. The views are mainly of the Mediterranean area, Syria, and the north of Cyprus. As is usual, the name of the pattern is printed on the reverse.

▶ **A platter by Robinson, Wood, & Brownfield,** *c.*1836–41
From the "Zoological" series, showing animals in zoological gardens, possibly Regent's Park, London. **£350–450/$525–675**

▼ **An open baking dish by John & William Ridgway,** *c.*1814–30 From the "Rural Scenery" series, an uncommon serial pattern. **£350–450/$525–675**

▲ **A platter by Ralph Stevenson,** *c.* 1810–35 (probably 1820–2) From the "Semi-China Warranted" series of rural scenes; marked "R.S." on the reverse. **£650–750/$975–1,125**

# Animals & Birds

In the early nineteenth century, public interest in animals and birds increased, fostered by the amount of literature available on the subject, and prompting potters to reproduce such subjects on their wares. Some of the first animals to appear on pots were the more exotic kind, such as the "Elephant" and the "Zebra" patterns made by Rogers, in both of which the animals are set in an incongruous Chinese-style landscape. This proved a popular alternative to the more usual "Chinoiserie" available at the time. Swansea also made a stylized elephant pattern, and Turner produced an early example of a man on an elephant holding a parasol.

Elephants also feature strongly in Spode's "Indian Sporting" series, this time all shown in their natural jungle habitat. Most of the Indian patterns also feature an elephant somewhere in the design. The popularity of this animal was largely due to the presence of one in the Zoological Gardens in Regent's Park – a novel and exciting sight at this time.

The "Grazing Rabbits" pattern is a firm favourite with many collectors; it is quite delightful, showing three rabbits grazing under a tree in a rural setting. There are giant primroses in the foreground almost the size of the rabbits themselves. The maker of the pattern is unknown at present, but it is possible that two different factories produced it: a deduction based on viewing a large quantity of pieces together and noting the variation in size and quality of the plates. The colour and care with which the transfer is applied is not consistent, though most pieces are excellent.

The series appears to be produced mainly on tableware and toilet items, with tureens that are rather plain in style but dessert baskets and a pierced stand that are stunning. The piece illustrated is part of a circular supper set that originally came on a fitted mahogany tray. Servants would leave a light meal in sets like this, for well-to-do families to eat after returning late from the theatre or other function. A rectangular set also exists in

▶ **A lidded segment dish from a circular supper set, *c*.1820** In the "Grazing Rabbits" pattern. Unmarked; of very high quality.
£470–550/$705–825

◀ **A tea bowl & saucer in the "Milkmaid" pattern, *c*.1820** Unmarked; this pattern was made by several factories.
£170–230/$255–345

this pattern, which supports the idea that the pattern was produced by more than one potter. Many of the other rural scenes by various potters include farm animals such as cattle, sheep, and goats. Some of the serial patterns have different animals on each item – a good example of this is the "Semi-China Warranted" series by Stevenson, one of which is the platter illustrated here, showing horses.

Perhaps one of the most famous, and some claim most desirable, animals to appear on pottery is the "Durham Ox", discussed earlier in the book (*see* page 18). The "Durham Ox" series includes eight known views, all sharing the same distinctive border of stylized flowers, and was produced by an as yet unknown maker. Items have appeared with both "Withers" and "Fell" printed on the reverse, but these are thought to refer to possible retailers rather than makers. The most famous image of this animal came from an engraving of 1802 by J. Whessel, after a painting by J. Boultbee, of *John Day with the Durham Ox*. The story is that the ox was

taken by Day to fat stock shows throughout the country. The beast grew so large that a special carriage was built to transport it, but after a period of six years it slipped and died, leaving a carcass weighing some thirty-four hundredweight. To some collectors, having a "Durham Ox" in the collection is the be-all and end-all, but there are arguably many more attractive items to collect.

The "Milkmaid" pattern produced on tableware by Spode is one of a number of variations of this attractive pattern, which was made by other potters and is more usually found on tea wares. It is very possible to use this theme as a basis for a collection, as it is suprising how many different styles are available. The quality of the print varies, however, Spode being the best.

Another very extensive series using animals is the "Quadrupeds", made by John Hall in the early 1820s; Dimmock and Smith of Hanley continued making the series in 1832, buying the copper plates after Hall ceased trading. The earlier Hall version is

▲ **A platter by Spode, c.1830** From the "Aesop's Fables" series, showing the "Horse & the Loaded Ass". Modern reproductions of this platter are available – remember to check the details on the reverse. £950–1,200/ $1,425–1,800

▲ **A soup tureen stand by Spode, c.1830** From the "Aesop's Fables" series, showing the "Fox & the Goat". **Perfect condition £450–550/$675–825; damaged £250–300/$375–450**

◀ **A plate by Spode, c.1830** From the "Aesop's Fables" series, showing the "Fox & the Lion". £150–190/$225–285

far superior however. As the name implies, the series depicts four-footed animals, some exotic, some British, and it was produced in a very dark blue – especially the Hall version (which would have been one of the reasons for its popularity with the American export market). Most items are marked with "Quadrupeds" and the maker's name, but not with the name of the animal pictured.

The "Arctic Scenery" series, produced by an unknown maker around 1835, shows Eskimos, igloos, dogs, and bears in an Arctic landscape. The borders vary, featuring exotic animals more suited to the jungle. Printed in a light to medium blue, the series is rare and thought to have been produced principally for the Canadian export market.

A series made by Job Meigh in 1837–40, called "Zoological Sketches", again shows mainly exotic animals but also includes a fox and badger. The border is very open and includes birds and scrolls. This is a good example of an early instance of the later, more open type of design which was favoured

after 1830. A pattern by Robinson, Wood, & Brownfield, produced in the late 1830s, shows zoo animals in a garden setting. It was made in a bright, almost turquoise, blue and has an unusual checked fabric-like border.

One of the most striking views involving animals is the "Lions" pattern by Adams, made around 1820, showing a majestic "king of the jungle" lion, a lioness, and cubs. Its source is Scott's *Felix, Leo, Lioness, and Young* from 1807, and the pottery was made around 1820. This pattern is fairly rare, the large platters achieving very good prices. Another lion scene is the "Angry Lion", made around the same time by an unknown maker. This depicts a dangerous-looking lion with his eye on two people who appear to be running away from him – another very impressive pattern. Enthusiasts have been known to collect anything showing a lion – even if it is just on the finial of a tureen lid. As we have seen, collecting can be very focused indeed!

▲ **A small plate by Spode, c.1830**
From the "Aesop's Fables" series, showing the
"Fox & the Grapes". **£250–300/$375–450**

▲ **A vegetable tureen by Spode,**
**c.1830** From the "Aesops Fable's" series,
showing the "Wolf & the Crane" and the
"Wolf & the Lamb". **£450–550/$675–825**

The "Aesop's Fables" series, introduced
towards the end of the Spode era and continued on
through the Copeland and Garrett period and
beyond, is a very endearing series that draws from a
selection of Samuel Coxall's *Engravings of Aesop,*
published in 1793. Some of these scenes are rather
cruel, and others amusing. Other colours in
addition to blue were produced – green seems to
have been the most popular, especially during the
Copeland and Garrett period, while black is quite
uncommon. The printing is usually excellent in all
colours. All the items are marked both with the
fable and the potter.

Herculaneum also produced a very limited
selection of Aesop's Fables views – usually on
smaller items such as tea and coffee wares, small
plates, and mugs, which are normally unmarked.
The animal is usually more prominent in the
picture, the fox being a favourite. Other unknown
potters also produced some items of lesser quality,
including nursery china.

# Collecting
# *"Aesop's Fables" series*

▲ **Backstamp from the "Aesop's Fables" series,**
**c.1830** A typical backstamp from this series, identifying
the tale and the maker inside a cartouche, with flowers
and foliage surrounding.

As illustrated above, the "Aesop's Fables"
series has a very decorative and distinctive
backstamp. Some of the pottery is impressed
with the Spode mark, which is done before the
initial firing of the biscuit clay. At this stage it is
not usually known which design the items will
finally carry, so they cannot be impressed with a
pattern name – some of the Copeland and
Garrett items have an impressed mark, but not
all. The underglaze mark giving the title of the
fable is printed at the same time as the pattern,
being applied by the transferrer on the underside when decorating the item. The tureens
have a separate fable on each part, as do jug and
bowl sets, and anything with a lid.

As the pattern was introduced at the end of
the Spode era, it is not unknown to find an
impressed Spode mark alongside an underglaze Copeland and Garrett mark. Some of the
printed marks also show that an attempt was
made to remove the Spode mark from the title
by covering it over with blue ink; and, as usual,
a few unmarked specimens do appear on the
market. Generally speaking, the blue of the
Spode version is softer than in the later
examples; those produced during the Copeland
period, after 1850, tend to be of a harder blue,
with less perspective in the pattern.

◀ **A circular fruit bowl made by Woods & Brettle, *c.*1818–23** Showing the "Bird's Nest" pattern, a very heavily decorated design. **£470–550/$705–825**

▶ **A large saucer dish by Spode, *c.*1820** Showing the rare "Oriental Birds" pattern. It is deep to allow the tea to cool before drinking it from the saucer. **£170–240/$255–360**

▲ **A dessert or cheese plate by Dawson, Sunderland, *c.*1830** Showing another version of the "Bird's Nest" pattern. **£150–240/$225–360**

Birds feature very frequently on pottery, some being depicted in a more "naturalistic" manner, while others are very stylized. The pattern entitled "The Goldfinch", by an unknown maker, is an example of a naturalistic design, whose source is an engraving from Thomas Bewick's *A History of British Birds*, of 1797–1804. The bird is perched on the branch of a rose bush, with a butterfly in the background. Roses and other flowers make up the border. It is more usually found on tea services and tableware. The background to the pattern is blue, giving the appearance of white on blue – an impressive effect. Other versions of this pattern are available but the decoration is not so true to life.

A number of patterns all sharing the same title of the "Bird's Nest" were made by different factories, the most frequently found version being by Dawson, the Sunderland pottery in production between 1825 and 1830. It shows a seated boy offering a bird's nest to a girl with a dog (it should be remembered that at this time the collecting of wild birds' eggs was perfectly legal, unlike the present day). This pattern is usually only found on small items or tableware. A previously unrecorded pattern by Edward and George Phillips of Hanley, Staffordshire, dating between 1822 and 1834, shows a bird's nest containing eggs. This can be seen on the cup and saucer illustrated, which were purchased in America and were therefore possibly produced for export only – a theory supported by the fact that the colour is a very dark inky blue. Another example of a bird's nest is shown on the fruit bowl made by Woods and Brettle, Staffordshire potters who worked for the short period of 1818 to 1823, after which Wood joined Edward Challinor to become Wood and Challinor. The bowl illustrated, showing a bird feeding her young, is from an extensive service all featuring the same design.

Other bird designs include the "Ornithological Birds" series produced by Stevenson, Minton, and an unknown maker, all at the beginning of the nineteenth century. This series shows various birds and stylized flowers and branches. Although most of the birds are British in origin the general appearance is one of an Oriental design, and it is quite open, with a lot of white visible. The series is

◄ **A plate by Ralph Stevenson & Williams,**
*c.*1825 In the "Beehive & Vase" pattern; printed in
very dark blue for the export market. These two
potters were in partnership only for a very short
time; marked in underglaze blue on reverse.
**£220–270/$330–405 with rare mark**

► **A tea bowl and saucer by**
**Edward & George Phillips,**
*c.*1822–34 In the "Bird's Nest"
pattern. With an underglaze blue
mark – the first marked piece
recorded. **£250–290/$375–435**

quite extensive, though examples are not that common nor indeed popular.

John and William Ridgway (1825–30) produced the "Oriental Birds" pattern, a single design found on many items, produced with an attractive moulded gadrooned edge typical of Ridgway items produced at this time. The pattern is of an open design – three birds perched on a tree with flowers at the base and in the border. It can also be found printed in brown as well as blue, and may have been produced in other colours. The shapes of the tureens and items from the dessert service are decorative and make a good dresser display.

Peacocks were a particular favourite, featuring in many designs, especially in the gardens of the later romantic patterns popular from 1840. Spode also used the peacock in an earlier design found mainly on tea wares. Mason made a pattern entitled "Blue Pheasants", showing three pheasant-like birds among large peonies and other flowers, which again has a "Chinoiserie" look because of the border. The pattern is printed on ironstone china, which is heavier than the usual earthenware. The glaze is very shiny and the blue bright in tone, and it is a single pattern rather than a serial one.

No discussion of the use of birds as decoration is complete without mention of the "Asiatic Pheasants" pattern made by so many factories from the late 1830s onwards, and still produced today. As it was produced mainly for the domestic market rather than for export, items do not tend to be marked "England" and so can be hard to date, as they cannot be positioned either side of 1891, the date from which export produce had to have the country of origin marked. Wedgwood and Co., at Tunstall, claim to be the original makers of the pattern, but this is not certain; the name of the pattern is often printed on the reverse, sometimes including the maker, but by no means always. This was the most popular pattern of the Victorian era for dinnerware, its clean, light colour, and design being much better suited to the oak and mahogany dressers then popular than the earlier "Willow".

Birds and animals are often less prominently featured in more general landscape and stylized patterns, too numerous to discuss here.

▶ **A rare custard cup by Edward Challinor, *c*.1840** From the "Oriental Sports" series; most of the designs were copied from the famous Spode "Indian Sporting" series, and the quality is not quite so high. £230–300/$345–450

▲ **A plate printed in green by Copeland, *c*.1890** From the "Field Sports" series. £50–65/$75–100

▶ **A plate attributed to Ralph Stevenson, *c*.1820** Showing the "Springer Spaniel" pattern. £150–240/$225–360

# Sporting Subjects

The broad category "sporting subjects" includes such pastimes as hunting, shooting, and fishing – both British and big game hunting. In 1820 Enoch Wood produced his extensive "Sporting" series. The pieces are usually marked with the maker's name, but not the type of animal being hunted. Serial in nature, each item in the pattern shares the same border of flowers within scrolls. It is printed in a dark blue, most probably for export; examples are uncommon in England. The patterns feature a mix of English and exotic animals, including ducks, deer, fox, leopard, hyena, polar bear, moose, tiger, zebra, whippets, and an elephant. The quality of the glaze is not always perfect, but this is well compensated for by the lively subject matter; and the foliage in most of the designs is rather large in scale in comparison with the size of the animal.

The previously discussed Spode "Indian Sporting" series must also be mentioned in this context, as it includes probably the most extensive and well decorated of all hunting scenes produced on pottery – it is in fact worthy of its own book, in which it could be discussed in greater depth.

The "Springer Spaniel" pattern was made by a Stevenson (probably Ralph Stevenson) in the first quarter of the nineteenth century. It shows a spaniel chasing after a game bird that resembles a snipe, and is a single pattern appearing mostly on tableware. The border is fairly wide, covering the edge of the plate and extending well into the centre, and composed of leaves and flowers, possibly primroses.

A later example by Copeland, "Field Sports", is a composite series of English hunting and horseracing scenes, possibly introduced only in the early part of the twentieth century. The series was made mainly in green, but blue and brown examples have been found. The shape of the tureens is stunning, particularly that of the soup tureen. Perhaps because of its fairly recent date of manufacture, which could mean that items have not yet appeared for resale, it is not the easiest series to find.

One well-known pattern is the "Gamekeeper",

► A rare plate by Enoch Wood, *c.*1820
From his "Sporting" series,
showing "The Dog & The Snipe".
£290–380/$435–570

◄ A plate by Copeland, *c.*1890
A further example from the "Field Sports" series.
£50–65/$75–100

which shows the protagonist of the title out with his dog, and Goodwood House (Sussex) in the background. This was an unattributed pattern until 2002, when a plate marked "Hackwood" appeared at a race course fair and is now in the hands of a delighted collector.

Sporting subjects can also include archery; Herculaneum produced a series featuring this pastime, as did Baker, Bevans, and Irwin of the Swansea pottery, Wales. Another by an unknown potter shows an archery lesson, which appears to be of early production. Baggerley and Ball of Longton in Staffordshire produced sets of storage jars in various sizes showing Robin Hood about to shoot an arrow from a bow.

Boxing is another activity that featured on pottery – one example occurs on a mug from the Enoch Wood "Sporting" series, which also shows hunting near Windsor, bull baiting, and cock fighting. Bull baiting is found in other patterns, as is bull fighting, which usually appears in the

"South American Sports" series produced in the second half of the nineteenth century by an unkown maker. Bell, the Scottish potter, depicted badger baiting as one of his sporting subjects, and must have reproduced other such topics.

The more animal-friendly game of cricket is featured in Goodwins and Harris's "View of Windsor Castle" from their "Metropolitan Scenery" series. The inclusion of the match is in fact a piece of poetic licence, as its source is *Grand Cricket Match played in the Lord's Ground, Mary-le-bone* (taken from the *Sporting Magazine* of 1793) – an entirely different location, and another example of the use of two separate source prints to form a picture. This scene appears exclusively on a 48cm (19in) platter, and as there was only one to a dinner service these are very rare and highly sought after by collectors.

Other sports that you may encounter include tennis and golf, but these are more often found on children's plates and other nursery items.

► **A very rare two-handled basket dish by Spode, *c.*1825**
This item uses the border from the "Jasmine" pattern. The beehive in the centre is believed to be the arms of a St John's College (ref. Spode Museum Trust). **£400–475/$600–715**

◄ **A heavily potted salt cellar by Copeland,** ***c.*1850** Impressed date to underside. Showing the arms of Christ's Hospital school, Horsham. **£90–140/$135–210**

# Armorial Designs

Armorial is the adjective used to describe something "of or relating to heraldic arms", referring to the granting of a heraldic crest by (in Britain) the College of Arms, London. Many wealthy families had their own crest or coat of arms, which was often used on items belonging to them – such as their prized dinner service. The original pattern books now in the Spode Museum at Stoke-on-Trent contain many examples of these; unfortunately not all are listed with the corresponding family name.

The British royal family has a crest for each member when they become of age at eighteen or twenty-one years. Most of the regiments of the military and navy have their own designs also. Great Britain also has a large number of trade associated guilds and livery associations, each with its own crest. The significance of most is fairly evident from the composition of the design, while others are more cryptic. An interesting series of cigarette cards showing the different guilds and liv-

ery companies of London was produced in 1913 by Wills. Entitled *Arms of Companies*, this resource for pottery images is in itself an interesting sideline to collecting pottery.

John and Richard Riley were commissioned in 1823 to produce a very extensive dinner service of one thousand five hundred and ninety pieces for the Drapers' Company of Coventry. All items had the company crest in the centre, and most had a border of flowers based on the Riley "Floral Basket" pattern, while some of the dessert items were made without a border. The cost of the service, including an engraving charge of £16, was £86 12s 6d (nearly £4,900/$7,350 today), calculated after a discount of fifteen per cent on direct orders. The service was delivered by canal using Pickfords, with a packing cost of £3 (£170/$255 today), including twelve shillings and six pence for the straw. Much of this service still exists today, and it was in use at formal functions until recently. A new reproduction service that can be put into the dishwasher was

► **A plate by John & Richard Riley, *c.*1828** Made for the Drapers' Company of Coventry. With the border from the "Floral Basket" pattern. Part of a very extensive service. **£140–170/$210–255**

◄ **An ironstone china plate by Hicks & Meigh, *c.*1806–22** Showing the arms of the Salters' Company, inscribed "*Sal Sapit Omnia*" – salt savours everything. The company is correctly known as "The Worshipful Company of Salters", London. **£220–290/$330–435**

made by Spode in 2003. The bill of sale for the original service is on display at Drapers' Hall in Coventry. Most of the remaining pieces, apart from a few selected items kept for display at the hall, are coming onto the market. The author has had the privilege of being approached in this connection. One wonders how many other large services are hidden away in other places: odd items appear on the market all the time, but a full service is very rare.

The Salters' Company of London must have had a very extensive service at one time. Single items from this pattern have appeared for many years, but never in great quantities. It was made by Hicks and Meigh before 1822, when the partnership changed to Hicks, Meigh, & Johnson. A plate is illustrated here, decorated handsomely and showing the crest within a border of flowers, made in the heavier ironstone china for which Hicks and Meigh are known. The mark on the reverse is equally impressive. The gadrooned border is often discoloured and does not seem easily cleaned by any

of the usually reliable methods. This may be due to the type of clay used originally, which led to the final glaze not adhering to the plate edges as well as it should have done.

Some armorial wares bear only a picture, such as the beehive illustrated on the Spode sweetmeat basket opposite, which uses the border from their "Jasmine" pattern. The design for this can be found in one of the Spode pattern books, where it refers only to "St John's College", with no indication as to which one, though it certainly does not to relate to any still-existing British college. Examples of this design are few and far between.

Armorial ware was produced for Christ's Hospital, an independent boarding school founded in 1552 for the poor of London, which moved to Horsham in the early twentieth century. At least three factories made this, Copeland and Garrett being the earliest, followed by Copeland, and then George Jones. The items are usually quite heavily potted – necessarily so given the nature of their use.

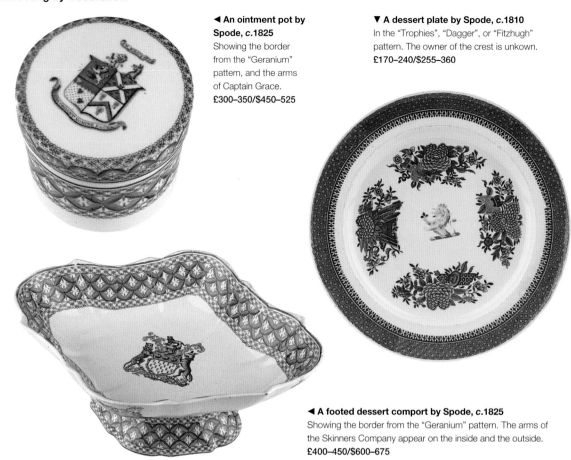

◀ **An ointment pot by Spode, *c*.1825**
Showing the border from the "Geranium" pattern, and the arms of Captain Grace.
£300–350/$450–525

▼ **A dessert plate by Spode, *c*.1810**
In the "Trophies", "Dagger", or "Fitzhugh" pattern. The owner of the crest is unknown.
£170–240/$255–360

◀ **A footed dessert comport by Spode, *c*.1825**
Showing the border from the "Geranium" pattern. The arms of the Skinners Company appear on the inside and the outside.
£400–450/$600–675

The individual dormitories were known as wards, and so some of the items are marked "Ward" along with a number. Some of the items are also inscribed "Christ's Hospital" under the crest. Examples with this pattern do turn up from time to time, the most common being pint mugs – presumably because they were produced in greater numbers. At least one collection with most of the numbers (one to ten) does exist, but this took many years to put together.

Mess plates made by the Bristol potters Pountney and Co. for use by the Navy, both at sea and in the mess rooms, have the number of the mess (the highest recorded being sixty-eight), and an attractive border of marine subjects. Queen Victoria's head is also included in the border, which tells us that they must date from after 1837, when she came to the throne. The later examples made by the Bovey Tracey pottery instead feature the head of King Edward VII. Some were also marked "chief petty officer" or other titles for non-commissioned ranks. Other pieces marked Copeland are also known. The bowls are very desirable as they have the mess number printed

upside down (on stormy waters it was more stable to store the bowls on their tops, which were wider than the base, and so the number had to be easily recognizable). Most items are also heavily potted, again in order to be sturdy enough for use on board a rocky ship. Some of the shipping lines and railways also possessed armorial wares, with the company name on the borders of their tableware; most of these are sparsely decorated, but they can form an interesting collection.

Items of toiletware, especially in the later dark blue "Tower" pattern produced by Copeland after 1880, can be found with the crest of Charing Cross Hospital in the border. The occasional item of medical ceramics, such as spittoons and invalid-feeding bottles, can be found with the same crest, which certainly lends an added interest to such a collection. Other items have the crest only on the reverse or the underside.

Spode must have produced a large selection of armorial designs, judging by the different items which have appeared. Most of these used only the border element from various patterns, the

**▲ A plate by Spode, c.1830**
"Prince of Wales Three Feathers & Gun Room",
with Union Wreath border. It is unclear as to
whom this armorial design belongs.
**£190–260/$285–390**

## Researching Armorial Designs

**▲ Armorial crest from Spode plate on left**
It is not always easy to discover who or what a set of
arms represents.

"Geranium" being quite popular. Others used were the "Nankin", "Jasmine", and "Union Wreath" patterns. Spode collectors prize these highly, especially if the crest is identifiable. Spode's vast pattern library holds various armorial designs, which are very interesting to see as they are all hand drawn, with handwritten notes. The information is sometimes fairly sparse, however – as we have seen, for example, regarding the St John's College thought to be represented by the beehive armorial.

Some troops of the British and Indian armies had the regimental badge in the centre or on the border of items in their dinner services, which were used for formal occasions. Collectors may prefer to begin with military armorial designs, as research is easier for this relatively public area than for private sources. The scope for collecting armorial designs is vast, however, and can be expanded to include all manner of items. Even today, the great factories are continuing to produce armorial wares for the home and export markets.

When researching the armorial design on a piece it can prove easier if you know the factory that produced it, as you may be able to approach someone there for information. Spode, for instance, has the Spode Museum Trust in the grounds of the Spode factory at Stoke-on-Trent (www.spode.co.uk); Wedgwood has its Visitors Centre in the Barlaston area of Stoke-on-Trent (www.thewedgwoodvisitorcentre.com); and the Potteries Museum in the Hanley area of Stoke (www2002.stoke.gov.uk/museums/pmag) is also useful. The Imperial War Museum in London (www.iwm.org.uk) may be able to help with military crests, and the National Maritime Museum with naval items (www.nmm.ac.uk). The Guildhall Library and the Museum of London (www.museumoflondon.org.uk) are also vast sources of information. Curators can be very helpful if you send them a picture. The reference section of public libraries is another potential source of information, and the staff are usually very helpful in pointing you in the right direction. Books have been written about the various trade and livery companies, which often give illustrations of the crests, and the Internet is another invaluable research tool. Finally, a basic knowledge of Latin is very useful in order to translate any inscriptions, which can provide vital clues.

▲ **A very rare bulb vase by Wedgwood,** *c.***1820** In the "Botanical" pattern. £400–550/$600–825

◄ **A foot bath jug,** *c.***1830**
Decorated in the "Lotus" pattern.
From Staffordshire, maker unknown.
£1,200–1,400/$1,800–2,100

► **Spode,** *c.***1820**
A very rare beehive
honey pot in the
"Chantilly Sprig" pattern.
£600–800/$900–1,200

# Floral Designs

Floral decoration is a vast category, and there are patterns to suit every taste. It can take the form of detailed depictions of individual identifiable flowers, often copied from a botanical print, or it may be stylized and fanciful in design.

Wedgwood produced their "Botanical" pattern around 1810, prompted partly by Wedgwood's personal interest in horticulture. The designs were taken from Curtis's botanical magazine: William Curtis published *The Botanical Magazine* from 1787 to 1800 (Volumes 1–14), and John Sims published *Curtis' Botanical Magazine* from 1801 to 1807 (Volumes 15–26). The Wedgwood pattern was serial in nature, each item having one or two flowers printed on it. The flowers on earlier pieces also have the number of the print at the base of the stem. Vast areas of white and a narrow border of concentric circles made for a very modern design, the later items having an attractive border of larger circles or convolvulus. Around 1830, Wedgwood produced another series, using their "Floral Basket" border

around a single botanical print. Some very interesting shapes were decorated in the Wedgwood "Botanical" pattern, including the very rare bulb vase illustrated. The shapes from the dessert services are simple but appealing, and this design is eye-catching when displayed in groups on a wall. Wedgwood also made the famous and sought-after "Water lily" and "Peony" patterns: the former is particularly stunning, with the flowers covering much of the object. The "Water lily" pattern was first printed in 1811, in brown, on a special service for Dr Robert Darwin, and then later printed in blue. It became very popular and continued in production for many years. The "Peony", though not so popular, also continued for some time. The "Hibiscus" pattern, originally produced about 1807 with an Oriental-style border, was not so popular.

Spode made a number of floral patterns, both single and serial in nature. One of the more unusual, and perhaps the rarest, is the "Floral" pattern, introduced at the end of the Spode period

◄ **Spode plate, *c*.1830**
In the "Floral" pattern. £170–190/$255–285

► **Ridgway, *c*.1825**
A side plate in the "British Flowers" pattern.
£120–140/$180–210

and made in blue and green, blue being the more popular. The border is unusual, as it appears to be white on blue rather than blue on white, and the shade of blue veers towards lavender. The centres, which are blue on white, are decorated using accurate representations of English flowers. A cartouche appears on the back, within which is marked "Floral", printed in the colour of the pattern. Other Spode serial patterns include "British Flowers", which is blue on white, and the "Botanical" pattern, which is the same pattern reversed – that is, white on blue but using the same designs. Both patterns continued into the Copeland and Garrett and Copeland periods, and are fairly sought after.

Spode made many single patterns, including "Geranium", "Jasmine", "Group", "Filigree", "Sunflower", "English Sprays", and the "Blue Rose". A group of designs called the "Union Wreath", contains four variations, with the rose, thistle, and shamrock either in the border or as the

central design. Further examples of floral designs were used for sheet patterns and other variations. Some of the more unusual patterns, such as "Daisy and Bead", "Honeysuckle and Parsley", and "Strawflower", are difficult to find. The "Daisy and Bead" is more often found on toy pieces, but is also available on larger items. Even now, new Spode patterns or variants from the norm are still being discovered. As with most Spode pottery, the quality of the pottery and the decoration is excellent; it is understandable that many collectors should choose to concentrate solely on collecting Spode.

John and William Ridgway made a very attractive pattern called "British Flowers", which seems to appear only on tableware. Another serial pattern, it shows a central flower with four union wreath groups in the border. The pottery is very white and the flowers are printed in a clear medium blue. Some of the dessert items have a gold rim, and the handles are made of a rose raised in relief and printed in a darker blue. Again, a group of plates in

▶ **A bombe-shape footbath by Minton, *c.*1830**
In the "Florentine" pattern.
£1,500–1,900/$2,250–2,850

◀ **A plate by Wedgwood, *c.*1820**
In the unusual "Botanical" pattern, with the "Floral Basket" border. £120–140/$180–210

this design make a very nice wall display – even minor damage is often not visible if the plates are high up. The underside is printed with "British Flowers Opaque China", and it was the distinctive shapes of both the dessert items and the tureens that led to the attribution to Ridgway, as well as the fact that "Opaque China" is a mark known to have been used by Ridgway. Ridgway produced other floral patterns, namely "India Flowers", and "Windsor Festoon", that were more stylized in design.

The Minton factory was another prolific producer of floral designs, many of them white on blue, which were popular for export. The patterns include "Botanical Groups", "Botanical", and "Floral Vases". All these patterns have the "Semi-China" mark in a hexagonal pseudo-Chinese box on the reverse, which is known to be a Minton mark. Two other patterns by this factory that also appear with this mark are "Leaf" and "Botanical Vase". All these patterns are very sought after. Minton also produced a version of the "Filigree" pattern made by Spode; the Minton version has a central basket of flowers, while the Spode version

has a bowl. The Minton pattern also has a sailing ship and semi-nankin printed on the reverse. A third, unknown, maker also produced the pattern.

The earliest of Minton's other floral designs is the "Basket" pattern, which has an Oriental feel, followed by the "Dahlia" sheet pattern. There is some discussion as to whether they may have produced a similar pattern to Wedgwood's "Botanical", but this has not been proved conclusively. The "Dresden" pattern appears with two differing borders, and the "Florentine" pattern, illustrated here, shows a vase and a serpent-like mythical beast. Another very attractive design is "Trellis and Plants", which has a border with a trellis and different flowers in the centre, depending on the item decorated. The "Lace Border" series has a border of lace interspersed with garlands of flowers.

Brameld, the notable Yorkshire pottery, made a very distinctive design known as the "Sweet Pea", showing sweet peas within a narrow border. This pattern is quite rare, as is the shape of the plates, which are eight-sided, with an impressed Brameld

▲ **A fluted dessert comport by Ridgway, c.1825** In the "British Flowers" pattern, with gilding applied to rose handles.
£150–170/$225–255

▲ **A dessert or cheese plate by Spode, c.1830** In the "British Flowers" pattern.
£140–160/$210–240

► **A sauce tureen, cover, and stand by Spode, c.1830** In the unusual "Floral" pattern.
£400–450/$600–675

mark on the reverse. Though not a sheet pattern, the white flowers on a medium to dark blue background do cover the whole object. Two other Brameld patterns are the "Twisted Tree" and the "Parroquet", which although also containing birds are mainly floral in appearance.

William Adams of the Greengates pottery made a stylized floral pattern, the "Tendril", early in the first quarter of the nineteenth century. This has a central design surrounded by flowers and tendrils printed in a dark blue, but is not as attractive as some of the other floral patterns.

John Turner of Lane End Pottery made an early floral pattern between 1810 and 1815, called the "Daffodil". It was very white, with small, sparse sprigs of flowers and four single daffodils printed on the edge making a fairly plain pattern.

The Rogers factory produced several floral patterns, the most flamboyant being "Fruit and Flowers", showing fruit and large flowers with an Oriental influence. The pattern is uncommon, and very busy – making it better suited to larger pieces.

Another fruit and flowers pattern, by Hicks and Meigh in the mid-1820s is much more English in design, including apples, pears, cherries, and spring flowers. It also has a gadrooned and indented edge, which adds interest.

The "Oriental Flower Garden", by Goodwin, Bridgewood, & Orton of 1827–9 and in a later, more romantic style of design, is a view of a garden with flowers, water, and a large urn. "Stylized Flowers", by the same maker, is a stylized geometric design using flowers and leaves.

Many sheet patterns use flowers or leaves as their theme, as these lend themselves more easily to the wallpaper-like covering of an object than other less abstract subjects. A separate border may then be applied. These patterns are found on toy items, infant feeding bottles, and pap boats, and the joins are often very noticeable, especially on the larger items. Other colours are available, in addition to blue, in many of the patterns, so floral pieces easily blend with most interior design schemes. Don't forget that a collection can actually be used, and may look wonderful on a table laid for dinner. The scope for collecting floral designs is endless.

# Collecting by Factory

▶ **A plate, *c*.1820**
Showing the "Durham Ox". Maker unknown. Some collectors focus on the unnamed factories. £500–550/ $750–825

## Create a focused collection by specializing in certain manufacturers

▲ **A pickle dish by Spode, *c*.1820**
Showing the "Italian" pattern. Spode seems to be the most popular choice of factory for collectors. £175–225/$260–340

Blue-and-white pottery was produced by a vast number of potters in Staffordshire, Wales, Scotland, and other parts of Britain. Some collectors choose to focus on a single maker or a small number of them, a decision that is usually not consciously made until they have collected a few items.

Spode seems to be the most popular with collectors, possibly because of the consistent quality, the variety of designs and shapes, and the long period of production (including his successors). Other potters also made a good range of items and designs, however, and a collection can just as easily take on a regional slant, if specializing in individual potters does not appeal.

Welsh pottery made by the Swansea and Glamorgan factories is very desirable; the early wares are typically of the "Chinoiserie" style. One of the early patterns is the very stylized "Elephant", with the animal featuring in a Chinese landscape. They also produced copies of some of the Spode patterns including the "Castle", "Bridge of Lucano", and "Italian" designs. A famous and sought-after pattern by Welsh potters is the "Ladies

of Llangollen", a single pattern that seems to be available only on tableware, made by both the Cambrian and Glamorgan potteries. It shows two ladies – apparently Lady Eleanor Butler and Miss Sarah Ponsonby – astride their horses, talking to an estate worker who is carrying a scythe. The setting is a rural landscape, supposedly in the Llangollen valley, and the house in the background is unidentified. The two ladies also appear on another pattern by an unknown maker. Another Welsh design is the "Pultney Bridge, Bath", quite a scarce pattern found most frequently on jugs – you may even find puzzle jugs in this pattern.

Scottish pottery is a worthwhile theme to consider. Bell, the Glasgow potter, produced a serial pattern in pale blue called the "Triumphal Car", which shows various animals pulling a chariot – the animal changes depending on the size of the plate. They also produced the "Warwick Vase" pattern among others. In general, the quality of the potting was heavier and thicker than some, and the decoration was largely romantic in nature. The Clyde pottery in Greenock made similar patterns.

◄ **A large platter by Henshall, *c*.1820**
From the "British Views" series, showing Compton Verney, Warwickshire. £1,400–1,800/$2,100–2,700

► **A lidded custard cup by Spode,**
***c*.1815** Showing the "Trophies Nankin" pattern. £180–240/$270–360

▲ **A platter by Davenport, *c*.1820**
From the "Cornucopia" border series. The dark blue indicates that it was made for the North American market. £650–750/$975–1,125

Transferware was also made in Tyneside and the north-east of England; Dawson from Sunderland produced the "Bird's Nest" and "Tea Party" patterns, both in a medium to dark blue and often found on tea wares. Sewell and Fell from Tyneside produced a certain amount of blue printed patterns, as did the Maling factory, which made a pattern entitled "Demon's Egypt".

Brameld of Swinton, near Rotherham, Yorkshire, and his Rockingham factory produced a range of blue printed pottery, the "Returning Woodman" being a particularly impressive rural scene enclosed by a narrow border. The plates, as with some other Brameld designs, are eight-sided – adding to the collecting interest. Another Brameld pattern is a view of the "Castle of Rocheforte", France. An interesting serial pattern was the "Don Quixote", which contained many different designs, and was made in blue, green, and black. This factory also made floral patterns.

Another Yorkshire producer was the Don pottery, who made the "Vermicelli" pattern illustrated on a flask on page 24 – an interesting

and rare pattern to collect. The design seems to appear on tea wares and smaller items. The "Named Italian Views" series, showing scenes in Sicily, Naples, and the Italian mainland, has a very ornate border with flowers and putti. The scenes are of the kind you would expect to encounter on the Grand Tour of Europe, the trip on which it was fashionable at the time for young gentlemen to embark. Each scene's title is printed on the front of the item. Joseph Twigg, also a Yorkshire potter, made his own versions of some of this series (marking some with "Twigg"), but they are of inferior quality. A collection of the two makers of "Named Italian Views" would show the difference in quality, so they ought not to be displayed together – a factor that should always be a consideration.

In terms of production quantity and history, however, Staffordshire is the heart of blue-and-white printed pottery. Many factories located themselves in this area, and the work of the principal ones has much to teach us about making wise collecting decisions.

► **"Caramanian" series sweetmeat dish by Spode, *c.*1815.** The print on this item is not taken from the same source as the other "Caramanian" items, but is classified as such by the border. This same print is found on a water jug. £400–500/$600–750

◄ **A double candle snuffer tray by Spode, *c.*1820** In the "Musicians" pattern. Both the pattern and the shape are extremely rare. £1,500–1,800/$2,250–2,700

# Spode

Spode, a perennial favourite with collectors worldwide, is consistent in its quality and variety of patterns and designs available, so that there is something for most tastes. The production of blue printed wares by this factory started in the late eighteenth century and continues to the present day. It was in production under the name of Spode until 1833, when it was bought and traded under the name of Copeland and Garrett. Then in 1847 it became Copeland, a name which continued until 1970, when the name Spode was again used to celebrate two hundred years of continuous production.

Unlike the work of some other factories, it is rare to see evidence of stilt marks (frequently caused by the small pieces of clay used to separate items during firing) on the front side of Spode pottery, and these can often detract from the over-all beauty of the item. Very few pieces of inferior or "seconds" quality left the Spode factory. With unmarked items it is easier to rule out Spode in the process of identification if the quality is inferior.

As with most factories, the early wares were made in a dark cobalt blue. The designs displayed a Chinese influence, and were composed of three separate sections – the centre or main pattern, a narrow inner border known as the "nankin", and the traditional outer border common to most patterns. The early patterns included temples, pagodas, and other Chinese-type buildings. One such early design is the "Buffalo", soon followed by the well-known "Willow", which was copied by many other factories. Early on, it was not uncommon for any Chinese-style design to be called "Willow", even when it did not contain the proper elements. Variations of the "Willow" pattern, such as "Buddleia", "Two Figures", "Long Bridge", and "Flying Pennant", all have the familiar bridge but differ in other ways. The "Long Bridge" pattern, also copied by other potters, has a stretched bridge, on top of which there are only two figures. The "Net" pattern, illustrated here on a rare ice pail, depicts pagodas and willow trees in

cartouches among Oriental flowers, with a net design in the centre. Another early pattern also produced by other makers, this design seems to be found only on table items.

The "Lanje Lijsen", also known as "Long Eliza" or "Jumping Boy", is a direct copy of a Chinese pattern, as (confusingly) is the "India" pattern. It is interesting to compare the Spode patterns with an original Chinese plate, as they are almost identical (as we have seen on page 14). The "Grasshopper" pattern, again in Chinese-style, made with two different borders, is a very stylized pattern. A very rare pattern, "Chinese of Rank", illustrated in the section on jugs on page 122, is taken from a Daniell print from *Picturesque Voyages in India by way of China* – a truly impressive pattern that would add interest to any collection.

"Woodman" and "Milkmaid" are the only two marked Spode patterns showing English rural scenes; two other very rare patterns are "Country Scene" and "Shepherdess": a marked piece of either

of these designs is yet to be discovered, however.

The "Musicians" pattern, illustrated here on a candle snuffer stand, is very rare. It may take twenty years to find just three items in this pattern! However, Spode produced items for just about every possible use, especially in the more common designs, so there is always the chance of finding fascinating shapes if not rare patterns.

"Gothic Castle" is a combination of many styles, showing a fairytale castle, Chinese figures, a bridge, and an oversized pot of flowers in the foreground; the border even contains African and European animals. This pattern is known to have been made by other factories. Although many of the Spode examples are unmarked, they can be distinguished from other makers' versions by the single line-type stilt marks on the reverse – other potters used the traditional three pin marks forming a triangle.

Designs with an Italian influence – "Castle", "Italian", "Tower", "Bridge of Lucano", and the "Rome" ("Tiber") pattern – are quite easy to find on

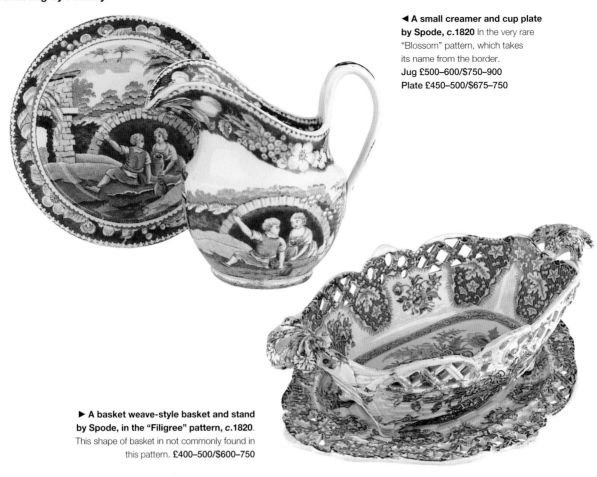

◀ A small creamer and cup plate
by Spode, *c.*1820 In the very rare
"Blossom" pattern, which takes
its name from the border.
**Jug £500–600/$750–900**
**Plate £450–500/$675–750**

▶ A basket weave-style basket and stand
by Spode, in the "Filigree" pattern, *c.*1820.
This shape of basket in not commonly found in
this pattern. **£400–500/$600–750**

plates and platters, but are less frequently encountered on the more unusual shapes. The other pattern with an Italian influence is the "Waterloo" or "Italian Church" pattern, which appears to have been used on tea wares and breakfast plates. The "Rome" pattern is perhaps the clearest of all the engravings produced by the Spode factory. Thomas Lakin also produced it in a version in which the circles in the border are larger, and the colour is darker, appearing dull in comparison. The Lakin pattern is unmarked, while the Spode version has an unusual mark that seems to be largely peculiar to this pattern – "Spode" is printed in underglaze blue within a blue frame.

The "Flower Cross" pattern shows, as the name implies, a cross of flowers, both horizontally and diagonally an attractive pattern for wall decoration. It is often unmarked, but always seems to have the traditional stilt marks of Spode. The "Lattice Scroll", again with a descriptive title, comprises latticework and scrolls of flowers. The "Lyre" pattern found on tea wares is a stylized interpretation of a lyre among flowers. The "Lily" and "Daisy" patterns are sheet patterns similarly found on tea items, as is the less scarce "Leaf" pattern.

The "Marble", or "Cracked Ice", pattern is relatively common; sometimes called the "Prunus" pattern, it is another copy of an early Chinese design, but made in a brighter royal blue. It is found on many different items, and has also been found printed in more than one colour.

The rare "Chantilly Sprig" pattern is illustrated on page 70, in the floral section; it is one of the few patterns without a definite full border, and was originally made on French porcelain, hence the name. The "Gloucester" pattern is of a similar style but has a narrow dark blue border.

Other patterns include the rare "Peplow" pattern, made in two versions, "Bowpot", "Fence", "Fruit and Flowers", and "Chinese Flowers", all with a Chinese influence. As has already been seen, floral designs are numerous. "Honeysuckle and Parsley" is an all-over pattern giving the appearance of white on blue. "Vandyke", which is found on tea wares, has a central spray of roses and an unusual border of bead-like decoration. Then there is

▶ **A shaped dessert dish by Spode, c.1830**
In the "French Birds" pattern.
£190–240/$285–360

◀ **An ointment pot by Spode, c.1815–20**
In the "Tower" pattern. £200–230/$300–345

"Daisy and Bead", often found on miniatures and toy items. Mention must also be made here of the "Starflower" pattern, a sheet pattern of starflowers on pieces with a gadrooned edge. The very rare "Blossom" pattern, shown here on a jug and a plate, and on a butter tub on page 120, features blossom in the border. Marked items are very rare, and collectors unaware of its importance could easily miss the pattern. Spotting something like this is one of the joys of collecting.

The "Indian Sporting" series, an extensive range of scenes from the jungle and surrounding areas and illustrated here on a sauce tureen, is widely collected (sometimes to the point of obsession) for the variety of interesting patterns and shapes available. The tureens display at least three different designs if the undertray is included.

The "Caramanian" series, showing architectural scenes from Caramania ("a part of Asia Minor hitherto unexplored", according to the heading for the volume of Luigi Mayer's drawings), is extensive. The shape of the plates and tureens was altered to be more uniform with other patterns; and for some reason the border is the same as that of the "Indian Sporting" series, showing jungle animals. The pattern is extremely popular with collectors, and source prints for both these series are eagerly sought, often to match an item of pottery in the collection.

The "Greek" pattern is a series of classical designs and motifs, such as urns, vases, and scenes from Greek mythology. It was introduced in 1806 to satisfy the growing public interest in classical design and to complement the associated changes in interior design (again influenced by those returning from the Grand Tour, who had seen such wonders as at Pompeii). The pattern was also made in other colours and can appear with clobbering.

Another major series produced towards the end of the Spode period and into that of Copeland and Garrett was "Aesop's Fables", as discussed earlier. As we have seen, armorial designs were also extensively produced by the Spode partnerships.

This factory, as an area for collecting, has much potential and several books have been devoted to the subject. The Spode collector is truly spoilt with an endless choice of patterns, objects, and resources.

◀ **A rare footbath by Minton,** *c.*1815–20
In the "Castle Gateway" pattern.
This appears to be one of the
smallest footbaths produced.
**£2,700–3,500/$4,000–5,250**

▼ **A miniature or toy washbowl by
Minton,** *c.*1820 In the "Floral Vase"
pattern. **£140–170/$210–255**

◀ **A toilet box by Minton,** *c.*1825
In the "Bamboo & Vase" pattern.
**£190–240/$285–360**

# Minton

The Minton factory was until the year 2000 a very under-researched subject area, especially in relation to its blue printed wares. This has now changed following the extensive research by Geoffrey Priestman and the subsequent publication of his book on Minton printed pottery (*see* Further Reading, page 153), which revealed new pattern names along with their sources. The manufacture of printed wares by Minton began at the end of the eighteenth century, using the type of "Chinoiserie" designs common to other potters. The "Willow" pattern, and the "Bridgeless" pattern (named the "Hermit" by Minton after the single figure in the doorway of a pagoda), were made in great numbers. Other Chinese landscape patterns, such as the "Chinese Garden" and "Fisherman" were also produced, to be followed by early floral patterns with a Chinese influence, such as "Pinwheel", "Basket", and "Lily".

Minton's "Roman" pattern is not unlike the Spode "Greek" pattern, but also contains some Masonic symbols in the border, and is often referred to as the "Kirk" pattern after the engraver of the source designs. The "Camel and Giraffe" pattern, based on an engraving by Bewick, shows the animals in a Chinese-style landscape rather than their usual habitat. The "Bewick Stag" is a favourite, showing an oversized majestic stag with other deer against the background of a European landscape. The "Castle Gateway" pattern, illustrated here on the small footbath, is found on toilet wares, and the "Ruined Abbey" pattern, thought to represent Kirkstall Abbey in Yorkshire, is not dissimilar in design. The beautifully decorated "Monk's Rock" is a serial pattern showing British landscapes, most of the sources for which are now known. The series is very popular with collectors, and the larger meat plates command very high prices.

The "Benevolent Cottagers", based on a painting of the same name, is now known to be a Minton pattern, though for many years the attribution was unclear. The printing and quality of this delightful pattern are superb. It shows a country scene of a

▶ **A rare wheel design puzzle jug attributed to Minton, *c.*1825** In a floral pattern. There is a small bird just visible inside the perforation on the lower part of the jug.
£2,500–3,000/$3,750–4,500

▲ **A platter by Minton, *c.*1825**
From the "English Scenery" series, showing Windsor Castle and the River Thames.
£700–850/$1,000–1,275

cottage and a woman with children offering food to a seated man. The border of auriculas and primroses is very fine. The "Maypole" pattern is found only on mugs, and the "Cottage and Cart" on small tea wares. Other designs found mainly on small items are the "Domed Building", "Farmyard Scene", and "Fallow Deer", all in a medium blue. The "Minton Miniatures" series is a complete toy service featuring many British views, with the name of the place usually printed on the reverse. This pattern is a good start for a collection of miniatures. "English Scenery", printed in a paler blue, is another extensive serial pattern found only on tableware, showing a range of buildings, churches, and castles, including Windsor Castle. Some of the shapes from the dessert service are interesting. A few of the pieces have been found with a specific Minton mark, though most are marked "English Scenery Semi-China", a recognized Minton mark. Known locations represented include Ripon, Worcester, Gloucester, Fonthill, Canterbury, Grantully Castle, and Faulkbourn Hall. This is a

wonderful series to collect, as it is fairly easy to find, and looks especially good on a dresser.

Minton produced various botanical patterns, some of the most impressive being white on blue, not unlike the Spode botanical patterns; most were produced on toilet items. Names include "Botanical Groups", "Botanical", and "Botanical Vase"; all have the "Semi-China" mark printed within a frame. Other floral patterns include "Filigree", "Florentine", "Flora", and "Corinthian".

"Chinese Marine", introduced around 1825 and produced for a very long time, shows various scenes set in a stylized Chinese landscape. It appears on tableware and toilet items, with the pattern name printed on the underside, with the letter "M". The "Italian Ruins" pattern depicts a large bridge spanning some water with a ruined building in the background. The unusual border features berry fruit, ears of corn, and leaves. It was also produced on tableware and toilet items, though dessert items seem to be more common today.

▲ A platter by Wedgwood, *c.*1815
Showing the stylized pattern "Bamboo & Fence".
£220–290/$330–435

► A pair of very rare plate lifters by Wedgwood, *c.*1815–20 In the "Peony" pattern, used to tilt a plate to allow the gravy to drain in the desired direction.
£250–350/$375–525 pair

# Wedgwood

The name "Wedgwood" is primarily associated for many people with the basalt and blue jasper wares, but the factory also made a variety of blue printed pottery. As previously discussed, the early botanical designs were popular, as were the "Peony" and "Water Lily" patterns. They also made later floral designs in a darker blue, almost resembling flow blue.

One of the only Middle Eastern views produced was "Absalom's Pillar", or to give it its correct name, "Absalom's Tomb". The pattern did not prove popular for Wedgwood and was used only on tableware. Designs with a Chinese influence include the "Chinese Vase", showing a prominent vase of flowers decorated with a Chinese figure within an Oriental landscape, and the "Bamboo & Fence", also known as "Chinese Garden" and "Blue Bamboo", which is illustrated here. The "Blue Claude" pattern, showing classical buildings in a harbour setting, from an engraving after Claude Lorraine, was popular and remains so today. It was

made in small quantities but over a period of many years, so is fairly easy to find. The "Chinese Landscape" pattern made after 1822 is as the name describes, but paler than many other Chinese views.

The "Crane" depicts the bird in an disproportionate floral pattern. One of the most abundant of the Wedgwood designs was the "Blue Rose" border series featuring English and European landscapes within a rose border. An unusual example is illustrated here, on a pot pourri vase showing the Rookery, near Dorking in Surrey. This same view also appears on plates, and more than ten variations are known, though few have been identified as known locations. None of the scenes has the place name marked, but all are impressed with "Wedgwood". Many of the patterns were copied by Rostrand, a Swedish potter in production during the latter part of the nineteenth century, who also copied other British patterns: his views are the same, but the overall quality is inferior. Beware of completely

**▲ A pair of candlesticks by Wedgwood, c.1840**
In a floral design. Pairs of candlesticks are not easy to find in perfect condition. £900–1,200/$1,350–1,800

## Wedgwood marks

**▲ Example of a Wegwood impressed mark**
Marks should be examined carefully to check for imitations. Here you can also see the workman's marks – they were paid by the piece (that is, per item "good from the kiln") and so marked all their own work.

unmarked pieces – they are not usually Wedgwood. One of the most impressive pieces in the series is one showing a "View of the Tower of London and the River Thames", found on soup tureens and footbaths.

Wedgwood produced many transfer-printed tiles, such as the very desirable "Months" series, which consists of a different tile for each month of the year, or the "Seasons" – each season being represented by a different figure head. Later patterns, introduced at the end of the nineteenth century, include "Fallow Deer", which had originally been made by Rogers in the early part of the century, and "Ferrara", which is very like the earlier "Blue Claude" pattern.

All Wedgwood production was very fine and the glaze shiny. Many unusual shapes were made, including the set of plate risers illustrated here. A good collection of Wedgwood could take some years to accumulate, but the thrill of the chase would make the waiting worthwhile.

The Wedgwood mark was copied and imitated by other factories hoping to gain recognition on the back of the former's well-known and respected name. William Smith of the Stafford pottery marked his wears "W. S. & Co. Wedgwood" until 1848, when an injunction from Wedgwood forced him to stop. He then simply introduced another "e", so making it "Wedgewood". This was a shame, as William Smith was a good and innovative potter in his own right, who did not need to trade on the back of other potters. "Vedgwood" was another name used by Smith's factory, but because this was less similar to the Wedgwood mark it did not lead to litigation.

Another mark created to deceive was that of the John Wedge Wood factory of Staffordshire. Many of their marks take the form of "J. Wedgwood" to create a confusion with Josiah Wedgwood – though the original Wedgwood never included the "J" in their mark. A further variation is the mark "John WedgeWood", where the gap is omitted between "Wedge" and "Wood".

From 1890 "England" was added to the marks, and in the early twentieth century this became "Made in England". This can all sound very confusing, but always examine backstamps and impressed marks very carefully as some are deliberately deceptive.

▶ **A platter by Ridgway, c.1825** From the "College Views" series, showing Peterhouse College, Cambridge. £700–800/ $1,000–1,200

▲ **A footbath jug by Ridgway, c.1825** In the "Italian Flower Garden" pattern. Note the mythical beast with splayed claws forming the handle. £1,700–1,200/$2,550–1,800

◀ **A cheese plate by Ridgway, c.1825** Showing Osterley Park, London. £90–140/$135–210

# Ridgway

The Ridgway family were potters in the Hanley area of Staffordshire in various partnerships from 1792 until 1858. During most of this time they made high-quality blue printed wares. Some of the earliest were the "Curling Palm", the "Chinoiserie Ruins", and the "Net" pattern, all of which are in the Chinese style that was common at the time. Many of these designs were unmarked.

The "Angus Seats" series was a very extensive series of British country house views, all of which are untitled but thought to originate from a collection of engravings by Angus, entitled *Seats of Nobility and Gentry in Great Britain and Wales*. More than a dozen views have so far been identified. The main view is set within an off-square frame in the centre of the piece, the border contains four vignettes each containing another view, and between these are large flowers. Most items are thinly potted with distinctive points on the edges. There may be around twenty different views in the series.

The "College Views" series made by John and William is a series of over twenty scenes, most of them fortunately identified. A view of Peterhouse College, Cambridge, is illustrated here.

The "Blind Boy" is an endearing country scene of a woman with a dog offering help to a boy who appears to be blind, with a cottage and hills in the background. Very few items in this pattern are marked. The "Cowman", attributed to Ridgway because of the distinctive shape of the tureens, shows a cow in the foreground, a man to its right, and a thatched cottage on the left. It is printed in a dark blue with a floral border. The "Mandarin Opaque" pattern shows Chinese figures within a stylized floral landscape, and may also be Ridgway to judge by the shape of the tureens – although several items have been found showing a Minton mark, so this remains a mystery.

Ridgway produced many floral patterns, the most naturalistic being the "British Flowers" pattern previously discussed. This pattern was also

**▲ A pair of candlesticks by Ridgway, c.1825**
In the "Italian Flower Garden" pattern. It is unusual to find
a pair of candlesticks, as so many have been damaged or lost.
£900–1,200/$1,350–1,800 pair

produced by Edward and George Phillips, but their version is paler in colour and composed of multiple sprays of flowers rather than individual stems. Garden scenes, such as the "Italian Flower Garden" pattern illustrated here on a footbath jug and pair of candlesticks, were also produced.

As we have seen, Ridgway produced American scenes in a dark blue for the export market – notably the "Beauties of America" series of around 1820. Slightly later productions, around 1830, included the "Oriental Birds" and "Chinese Temple" patterns. Items in this pattern were made in an unusual eight-sided shape, with gradooned edges, including the tureens. More stylized patterns with a greater percentage of white showing, they proved popular because of their decorative shapes rather than their patterns. The "Oriental" series shows an Eastern scene with an elephant in the foreground, and like some of the other patterns was available in other colours – especially brown.

# Collecting
# *"Stafford Gallery" series*

**▲ A platter by Ridgway from the "Stafford Gallery"**
**series, c.1820** An extensive yet uncommon series.
£600–750/$900–1,125

The extensive "Stafford Gallery" series consists of more than ten rural scenes within a floral border. It seems to appear only on table items; an infant feeding bottle with the pattern is known to exist, but non-table items are extremely rare and this may be the only one.

The title "Stafford Gallery" is printed on the reverse, but not the name of the scene. One of the scenes featured, called "Rough Sea", shows an angry sea dashing on to some rocks at the base of a cliff. This view appears on a cake stand and does not blend well with the others owing to its maritime, rather than rural, nature. The other views so far recorded include "The Signpost", "White Horse", "The Trio", "The Old Oak Tree", "Peasants' Picnic", "Shooting and Fishing", and "Duck Shooting" – all more typical landscape scenes.

The designs all contain great detail, which means that the initial engraving must have been quite a lengthy task. It is not a common series – a dealer may find only one piece a year. For some reason the pattern has a limited appeal, despite the fact that the scenes are all attractive. This may be because the blue is paler and not so vibrant as some other patterns. It still makes a pleasing addition to any collection, especially if Ridgway is the main theme.

▶ **A small match pot or spill vase by Davenport, c.1830**
Oriental design; not a full pattern.
£190–210/$285–315

◀ **A platter by Davenport, c.1820**
From the "Rustic Scenery" series. £400–550/$600–825

# Davenport

Davenport was a partnership from the Longton area of Staffordshire, spanning nearly one hundred years. As with most potters who made blue-and-white printed wares, their earliest designs were in the "Chinoiserie" style. "Chinoiserie Ruins" is the earliest, followed quite closely by the "Bridgeless Willow" pattern. "Bisham Abbey", sometimes called "Tudor Mansion", was designed in a Chinese style despite being based on a large house by the Thames in Berkshire, which is now a famous sports stadium.

The extensive "Fisherman" series is both interesting and rare. It shows one or more people fishing, against a background of ruins. The trees framing the ruins remain constant in every design, as does the border. This series appears on both dinner- and dessertware. Davenport made some splendid rural patterns, mostly including farm animals and buildings, and some showing a watermill. One of the most extensive is the serial pattern "Rustic Scenes". Unlike many of the other

serial patterns produced, different scenes were used on plates of the same size. They all share the same floral border, with the pattern fully covering the plate in a medium to dark blue: a dresser filled with this pattern is quite stunning. The shape of the tureen is fairly plain, but the pattern amply compensates for this. "Rural Scenes" is very similar to the "Mare and Foal" series, also by Davenport, in which the mare and foal feature in an English landscape setting. These patterns blend well together, being of similar colour and design, and the shapes of the tureens are also the same. The "Villagers" shows a group of three people and a dog in a rural setting, with a boy playing a pipe. It is an attractive single pattern that appears on dinnerware and toilet items.

Some dark blue designs were produced for the American market, such as the attractive "Cornucopia" border series, showing pairs of cornucopia and large flowers in the border. The central scenes vary, but are all of a landscape nature.

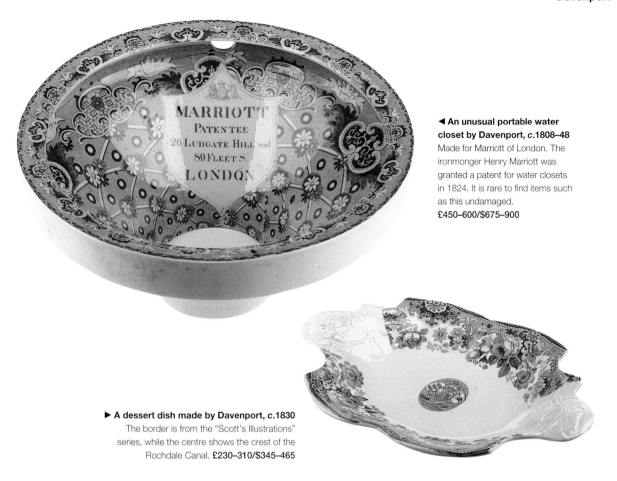

◄ An unusual portable water closet by Davenport, c.1808–48
Made for Marriott of London. The ironmonger Henry Marriott was granted a patent for water closets in 1824. It is rare to find items such as this undamaged.
£450–600/$675–900

► A dessert dish made by Davenport, c.1830
The border is from the "Scott's Illustrations" series, while the centre shows the crest of the Rochdale Canal. £230–310/$345–465

The "Mosque and Fisherman" is the only pattern to show an Indian scene, but should not be difficult to find as it was produced in considerable quantities on most items.

Davenport made many romantic-style scenes of European landscapes. "Rhine Views" is a serial design, the centre always having a different view, and the border giving the appearance of being solid colour whilst being composed of small wavy lines. Also in this style are "Swiss Chalet", "Tyrol Hunters" and "Views in Geneva". "Muleteer" is a pattern printed in a paler blue, showing a man with a mule in a romantic European landscape, with a border of distinctive large scrolls. The pattern was extensively used on toilet and medical items, and was also produced in a multi-coloured version.

"Scott's Illustrations" is an extensive series featuring scenes from Sir Walter Scott's work. The patterns include "Bride of Lammermoor" in two versions, "Legend of Montrose", "Heart of Midlothian", and "Waverley and Rob Roy". The pattern is printed in a paler blue and the name of the scene is printed on the reverse. It is wise to take your time when choosing a piece, as the quality of the printing on this design is not always up to standard.

Davenport also produced some floral patterns, the two most notable of which are the uncommon "Vase of Flowers" – a very decorative design of a large vase of flowers covering the entire surface of the object, with several different designs for the vase – and "Vase on a Wall", another decorative design featuring a vase of flowers on a wall in a garden setting. The latter pattern was rarely seen a few years ago, but quantities have appeared from mainland Europe recently, which suggests that they were originally produced for export to Europe.

There are many other designs made by the Davenport factory, and most appear to be marked with the maker's name. The rare portable lavatory pan illustrated above displays an example of a sheet pattern made by Davenport.

◄ **A platter by Riley, *c*.1820**
From the "Large Scroll" border series,
showing Denton Park. **£600–750/$900–1,125**

▼ **A platter by Rogers, *c*.1820**
Showing the "Fallow Deer" pattern. This pattern
was reintroduced by Wedgwood in the early
1900s. **£350–450/$525–675**

◄**An unusual divided sweetmeat dish by Rogers, *c*.1820**
Showing the "Fallow Deer" pattern. **£300–350/$450–525**

# Riley & Rogers

John and Richard Riley made a selection of wonderful blue printed wares in the Burslem area of Staffordshire from 1802 to 1828. Most of their output was devoted to items for the table, including dinner- and dessertware. Most, but not all, were marked with the factory name. One of the most notable and extensive services made was for the Drapers' Company of Coventry (*see* pages 66–67).

The "Eastern Street Scene" is the only example of an Indian view, taken from a Daniell engraving, while a scene after Claude Lorraine is the only view of continental Europe – taken from an original painting by the seventeenth-century artist. The latter scene was also used by other potters. A good example of one of the less expensive rural landscape patterns to collect is "Europa", featuring a lady mounted on a bull in a typically English rural landscape and found mainly on table items. A similar pattern is the "Girl Musician", in which a girl plays a pipe with another girl and a herdsman nearby, all set in front of a large house in a rural landscape. As with

the "Europa" pattern, the border is floral. These two patterns blend well together and are of similar value. The only serial pattern made by Riley is the "Large Scroll" border series (see feature box opposite).

The Rogers partnerships (John & George Rogers from 1784 to 1815, and John Rogers & Son from 1815 to 1842) made pottery in Longport, Staffordshire, and their production of blue printed wares was extensive. Their early designs – the "Monopteros", "Camel", and "Musketeer" – are all based on Daniell prints. As we have seen, "Elephant" and "Zebra" both feature the animal in an incongruous Chinese landscape. A pattern later copied by Wedgwood in the early twentieth century is "Fallow Deer", showing two deer in a snow-covered landscape, with a floral border featuring primroses and crocuses. "Rogers Views" is a series of English landscapes printed in a pale blue, with over a dozen different views within a floral border. Elkin and Knight made a similar series with their "Rock Cartouche" series. Most of the Rogers examples are impressed

**▲ An unusual bowl by Riley, c.1820**
Showing the "Feeding the Chickens" pattern. The bowl is marked "Riley" in underglaze blue. £400–500/$600–750

**◀ A dessert plate by Riley, c.1820**
From the "Large Scroll" border series, showing Canon Hall. £180–230/$270–345

# Collecting Riley's "Large Scroll" border series

**▲ Detail of the border from the "Large Scroll" border series, c.1820** From the platter opposite, showing Denton Park.

with "Rogers" but not the name of the place featured, some of which still remain unidentified.

The "Drama" series shows scenes from various plays, with the name, act, and scene printed on the face of the item. Pountney and Goldney copied the series, but you can tell the difference from the border – the Rogers version includes a masked face while the Pountney and Goldney one does not. Rogers also marked the piece "Rogers", while both have the pattern name printed on the reverse. The "Boston State House" pattern appears to be the only one made for the American export market, printed in a dark blue.

A fairly uncommon pattern, "Britannia", shows a seated Britannia facing two flags, one of which has "reform" printed on it, a girl kneeling beside a cornucopia, and an artist's palette in the foreground. At the top is an eye from which rays of light radiate. The border contains the union wreath motif, a trident, and a flag on a pole. Later Rogers patterns were European landscapes, including such locations as Athens, Florence, and Tivoli.

This is a wonderful series made by Riley, showing numerous British views surrounded by a border of large scrolls. The source for most of the designs was John Preston Neale's *Views of the Seats of Noblemen and Gentlemen in England, Scotland, Wales, and Ireland*. The dark blue colour again indicates that it was made for export to North America, where it went in great quantities. Much of it is now returning. The style and quality are very good, and it remains popular with collectors. Many of the houses featured are still standing today.

The pattern name is printed on the reverse, but not all have the name of Riley included – there is some debate as to whether the unmarked items are the product of the Riley partnership at all, and this remains uncertain. The copper plates for the design *may* have been sold and used by another potter after Riley went out of production, as they would only have had to alter the backstamp. This theory is supported by the fact that the usual Riley mark was replaced by the word "Warranted". Also, any marked "Riley" tend to be of a deeper colour with a crisper quality to the transfer. By the time another potter came to be using the plates, the engraving would have become thin from wear.

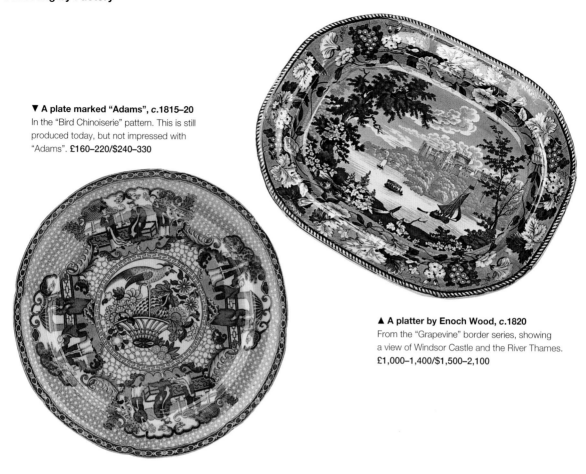

▼ **A plate marked "Adams", _c._1815–20**
In the "Bird Chinoiserie" pattern. This is still produced today, but not impressed with "Adams". £160–220/$240–330

▲ **A platter by Enoch Wood, _c._1820**
From the "Grapevine" border series, showing a view of Windsor Castle and the River Thames.
£1,000–1,400/$1,500–2,100

# Enoch Wood & the Adams Family

The skilled and prolific Enoch Wood partnerships of Burslem in Staffordshire were in production for over sixty years, running from 1784 to 1846. Founded by Enoch Wood, it was continued by his family as Enoch Wood & Sons. They were the largest British exporters of blue printed pottery to America, and so their wares include include numerous American views printed in the popular dark blue of the time. British scenes were still produced, of course, notable examples being the "London Views" series, printed in dark blue and so also popular for export, and "English Cities". The "Shell" border series features English and American scenes. There was also a "French" series in dark blue (presumably for export to France), and an Italian scenery series.

The "Grapevine", with its decorative border of grapes, vines, leaves, and convolvulus-type flowers on a stippled background, has an inner (or nankin) border of a twisted vine. The name of the place pictured is printed on the reverse, where the maker's name is impressed . This series is the most extensive serial pattern produced on any pottery, closely followed by the popular "Sporting" series – and both were most probably produced for export.

Two other patterns made for the export market, both very darkly printed, were the "Scripture" series showing biblical scenes, and the "Cupid" series featuring cherubs and flowers – both very "all-covering" patterns. "Lafayette at Franklin's Tomb" and the "Four Medallions" series were other export wares. One of Wood's many historical scenes is "Landing of the Pilgrim Fathers at Plymouth Rock" – a desirable pattern as it has the inscription on the front of the piece.

The name "Celtic China" was often included in the backstamp, to indicate that Welsh clay was used in the manufacture of Wood's wares – the "Grecian" pattern is one known to have this mark. The later years of production saw romantic-inspired patterns such as the "Belzoni" pattern, showing a series of mostly continental European

◀ **A rare lidded pot, possibly a slop pail, by Enoch Wood & Sons, *c.*1820** Showing "Lanercost Priory". "Wood" is impressed underneath, which is rare.
£1,500–2,000/$2,250–3,000

▼ **A plate by Adams, *c.*1830**
Printed in pink, showing the "Fountain" pattern.
£80–120/$120–180

hunting scenes, the "Fisherman" series, and the "Fountain" pattern, printed in all colours.

The Adams family first produced blue printed pottery in the latter part of the eighteenth century, their wares then being mostly "Chinoiserie" in design and unmarked. Adams also made a large amount of pottery for export to America, with many floral patterns in the typical dark blue. An interesting point is that the pattern was white on blue, lifting the design off the background and creating a lighter feel. An extensive series of London views was produced in this style, featuring the various Regency villas in and around Regent's Park.

"Flowers and Leaves" is an extensive border series featuring more than twenty-five different sites, the name of which are usually marked. The "Bluebell" border series was made with an identical border by both Adams and Clews, also using the majority of the same views. The Adams version is in a rich dark blue, which was presumably more favoured by the export market,

and most are marked with the name of the place pictured. A "Lorraine" pattern was also produced, showing an Italian landscape after the style of the famous painter.

The "Bird Chinoiserie" plate illustrated, which is sometimes referred to as "Chinese Bird", is a good example of an early pattern reproduced in 1910 and again in 1974. The original pattern is impressed "Adams. Introduced in 1799 at the Greengates Factory, Tunstall". When the pattern was reintroduced in 1910, the backstamp stated that the pattern was "introduced by William Adams in 1780 being a copy of an original Chinese design, Registration applied for". Since 1913, all items in this design have had the registration number 623295, because the pattern was patented including the backstamp. This causes confusion for many collectors. It should also be noted that the early items are lighter in weight, and that there is evidence of blue in the glaze on the underside.

◀ **A plate by Hicks & Meigh, *c*.1830**
Showing the "Exotic Birds" pattern.
**£70–130/$105–195**

▶ **A plate by Mason, *c*.1830**
From the "College" series; the college shown
here is unidentified. **£120–170/$180–255**

# Mason's & other Ironstone China

The Mason partnerships produced pottery at the Fenton Works, in the Lane Delph area of Staffordshire, from 1813 to 1854. Many collectors associate the name "Mason" with their brightly coloured and heavily gilded wares rather than with blue-and-white, but they should not be overlooked.

William Mason produced the famous "Beaded Frame" series, showing views of the British Isles within a floral border – a view of Richmond is illustrated on page 50; other views include Lynmouth, north Devon; Kirkham; Linlithgow Palace, Scotland; Monmouth; and Powder Mill, Netley Abbey. The name of the place featured is printed on the reverse within a beaded frame. A popular series, it can be found with or without the coloured clobbered border. Mason also produced views of Netley and Furness Abbey combined as a single pattern. A very attractive and rare pattern is the "Windmill" pattern – a pastoral scene with a windmill in the background. William later left potting and became a retailer in

Manchester, so items marked "W. Mason" are rare.

G. M. & C. J. Mason (George and Charles) continued in production longer than William. Their marks include "Mason's Cambrian Argil", impressed, and "Semi-China Warranted", printed in two lines – which both refer to the mix of the clay. The other more common mark is "Mason's Patent Ironstone China", either printed or impressed: Charles Mason developed this hard, white, durable pottery and patented it in 1813. An example of a design with the "Semi-China Warranted" mark is the "Trentham Hall" pattern, showing a large fountain in front of the Staffordshire house that was later demolished. A particularly attractive and rare pattern also bearing this mark is "Opium Smokers", showing men smoking long pipes in front of a large pagoda within a Chinese landscape.

A "Willow"-type pattern called the "Two-Man Willow", illustrated here on a vase, is quite common as it was produced over a long period, and it often appears in interesting shapes. An Oxford and

◀ **A vase by Mason, *c*.1870**
Showing the "Two-Man Willow" pattern.
**£250–300/$375–450**

▲ **A coffee can by Mason, *c*.1820**
Showing the "Dragons" pattern, often referred to as
"Chinese Dragons". A very common pattern found on toilet
wares in particular. **£190–250/$285–375**

Cambridge college series was also produced, though this was not as extensive as the Ridgway version. Mason's numerous other patterns are a field of their own that deserves to be studied in greater depth.

Ironstone china was also produced by other factories, some trying to mimic the Masons' wares, others using original designs. This heavier and glossier china was durable enough to stand up to the rigours of daily use, and did not chip as easily as the finer pottery. The Ashworth Brothers continued producing "Mason's" china, using some of the original moulds and keeping the name, though often with the addition of "Ashworth". Thomas and John Carey of Lane End, Staffordshire, produced the "Cathedral" series in ironstone china, showing British cathedrals, bordered by ecclesiastical motifs including a bishop's mitre. The Careys described their china as "Saxon Stone China". Cork and Edge of Burslem made stoneware that was not very different from other earthenware. This factory made many printed patterns in blue and other colours,

though the quality of the engraving was often poor. Davenport and Spode also made stone china in blue and polychrome, the quality of which was excellent.

Hicks and Meigh (1802–22) produced an extensive array of blue printed wares on stone china. Very little was marked with the maker's name, most having a Victorian coat of arms with the words "Stone China" and a number printed below – the numbers appear to signify the pattern. The partnership continued from 1822 to 1836 as Hicks, Meigh, & Johnson, still using the "Stone China" backstamp, this time in an eight-sided shape, with the number below. The quality produced by both of these partnerships was very high, with inventive shapes – especially for dessert items. Some of the patterns had a Chinese feel, others were floral with exotic birds, and the polychrome patterns closely resembled Mason's style. Charles Meigh (1835–49 and 1851–61) made patterns in a similar vein to Hicks, but the items were usually marked with the potter's name.

# Collecting by Use

## Endless variety in shape and purpose can inspire equally as well as surface design

▲ **An impressive soup tureen, cover, and undertray by Stevenson, *c*.1820–5** In the "Semi-China Warranted" series, showing a rural scene. £2,000–2,500/$3,000–3,750

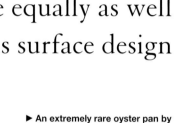

▶ **An extremely rare oyster pan by Spode, *c*.1820** In the "Italian" pattern. The exact purpose of this shape was discovered by studying the pattern records at Spode. £2,000–3,000/$3,000–4,500

# Dinnerware

To understand why so many items for the dining table were produced in the nineteenth century, we must remember that eating habits were very different from today. In prosperous households, dinner was an important social occasion for all the family, starting about two o'clock in the afternoon and continuing until at least five. Consisting of a minimum of three courses, and usually many more, it was a very substantial meal. Children did not eat with their parents, but stayed in the nursery. The middle and upper classes employed an army of servants, who often lived in the house in separate servants' quarters. Food was not taken to the table on plates, but rather in a variety of tureens and serving dishes made especially for the purpose. A standard dinner service in Georgian or early Victorian times consisted of forty-eight dinner plates, twenty-four soup plates, and twenty-four graduated plates (that is, a full range of sizes). To this were added a set of graduated carving dishes, a soup tureen with

underdish and ladle, a minimum of four covered vegetable dishes, open serving dishes, four sauce tureens (with under dishes and ladles), and gravy boats. Extra items included well-and-tree carving dishes, knife rests, salt cellars, mustard pots, asparagus servers (with accompanying butter boats and butter dishes), and separate long fish or salmon platters often with their own drainers – and this was just for the main courses: dessert was served on a range of different shaped dishes.

For most collectors plates and platters form the backbone of their collection, especially if displayed on a dresser. Once you have this background, the other shapes can soon be fitted in. Plates are graduated in size from about 12.5cm (5in) to 25.5cm (10in) in diameter. Children in the nursery used the smallest plates. The dished plates usually came in three sizes, the soup plate being the largest. When collecting plates, condition is of the utmost importance, as plates were produced in vast numbers and so there is more likelihood of finding

▶ **A pair of knife rests, *c*.1820** Showing an unknown border pattern only.
£190–220/$285–330 pair
£70–80/$105–120 individually

▼ **A plate, *c*.1820**
From the Staffordshire area; showing "The Boy Piping". Maker unknown.
£90–140/$135–210

▲ **A salad bowl by Stevenson, *c*.1820**
From the "Semi-China Warranted" series, showing a rural scene.
£550–650/$825–975

perfect ones. There may be knife marks and scratches, and soup plates can be very stained from the large amount of hot fat in the soup. Stains can be cleaned professionally, and it is wise to do so. Even judicious cleaning with abrasives and household cleaners can harm the pottery. Scratches can only be hidden with restoration, after which the item cannot be used. Unless the plate is very rare, always try to find a perfect example.

Platters, or ashets as they are known in Scotland, or even chargers, are available in graduated sizes – the largest usually 50cm (20in) to 56cm (22in) wide. They were available up to 69cm (27in) wide on special order from some potters. The particularly large platters would not have had a separate copper plate engraved specially for the size; rather the print for the largest regular size was used and the gap patched with pieces of transfer to give an all-over pattern. Sometimes the larger items had a double border to fill in the space instead. The weight of the very

large platters even when empty is considerable, but loaded with food they are weighty work indeed!

The largest meat dishes were usually limited to one only per dinner service, and are viewed differently from plates in terms of how you collect them. Condition is important, but unless they are for use, restoration is more acceptable. Platters were often stained by hot fat and fatty gravy – again this can often be cleaned, though not always. You should be aware that the stain may not be fully removed. Rust or ironmould stains from the non-stainless steel cutlery hardly ever come out completely. Cutlery was liable to rust, especially if the carving set was left lying in the gravy on the plate for any length of time. A drainer, often called a mezzanine, which fitted one of the larger platters, was used to drain the meat juices, or to keep fish flat. A long thinner platter known as a fish or salmon dish, often with its own drainer, was available as an extra. Because of their more specialized nature not so many were made, and so

◄ **A large fish platter 63.5cm (25in) in length, by Brameld, *c*.1825** The "Returning Woodman" pattern. These plates are rare as they were only available on special order from the factory. **£2,500–3,000/$3,750–4,500**

▼ **A soup plate by Heathcote, *c*.1820** With an impressed maker's mark. Showing Willersley Castle, Cromford, Derbyshire, from an engraving by R. Arkwright. **£160–220/$240–330**

◄ **A well-and-tree platter by Andrew Stevenson, *c*.1820** In the "Rose" border series, showing Walsingham Priory. **£900–1,200/$1,350–1,800**

good ones are quite difficult to find. A particularly fine one is illustrated above. Another "draining" platter was the "well-and-tree", so called after the shape of the troughs in the base that would funnel meat juices along "branches" and into a "well" at one end of the dish.

Tureens were made in various sizes, according to their intended use. The largest are soup tureens, sometimes made in two sizes, which were available with or without a matching ceramic ladle. Some families used a separate silver ladle, so the lack of a ladle does not necessarily mean the item is incomplete. An undertray or stand was essential for catching the drips. These were either like the platters, or more like a tray with handles and a recess for the base of the tureen. The smaller sauce tureens are usually the same shape as the soup tureens, but at least four were used at the same time; again the ceramic ladles were available only as an extra.

Covered vegetable tureens, usually numbering four, were of a simpler, larger, flatter design. Some were made in three parts with an under container

for hot water to keep the food warm. Some even had a draining plate, which fitted into the base to prevent the vegetables from becoming soggy. Open vegetable dishes, sometimes referred to as open baking or hash dishes, are also available. These were sometimes supplied with large domed lids that also fitted some of the medium platters, but they are rarely found today as their shape makes them vulnerable to damage, and they are often stained from oven use, especially on the underside. These lids look very attractive displayed on the pot board of a dresser. Salad bowls, either square or round, often stained from the use of oil, sometimes formed another element of the set. Gravy boats usually came in pairs and also had an undertray. Pay particular attention to the area at the base of the handle for signs of damage, as well as around the spout area.

Oyster pans were very rare, and were used to serve oysters at the table. Although oysters were a relatively common food at the time, available in rivers such as the Thames, only the very wealthy would have had pans such as this. They were

▼ **A plate by Henshall, *c*.1825**
Showing Guy's Cliff, Warwickshire.
£120–170/$180–255

available in several sizes and are very similar to dairy pans, which are usually round with a sloping, rather than a straight, side. Indeed, in the case of the oyster pan illustrated on page 94, it was only by looking in Spode's pattern book of 1820 that its non-dairy purpose could be confirmed.

Salt cellars, pepper pots, and mustard pots were placed at regular intervals around the table, each serving about four people. Not everyone used ceramic cellars, preferring instead to use the family silver. Ceramic knife rests were available singly or in pairs for the carving set, as were plate lifters, used to tilt the plate to allow the juices to be spooned up. These smaller items were frequently lost because of their size. Mustard pots are difficult to find with their lids, and even rarer with their original ceramic spoon.

The centrepiece of the table might have been a magnificent ice pail, such as the one illustrated here. In four parts, it comprises the lid, the top, a liner – usually undecorated and shaped like a pudding basin – and the base. These items are normally of a very decorative design, and are also very rare –

complete ones being particularly difficult to find. The ice, which was was held in the base of the pail, was often not very clean, having been collected from frozen rivers and lakes during the winter months and then taken by horse and cart to the house. Most large houses had an ice house, which was an underground cavity with a brick building above, used for storing the ice until it was required on the table. It was an indication of a family's wealth if it had its own ice house. The pudding-shaped bowl fitted inside, above the ice, and would hold whatever food needed to be kept cool. The top part would hold more ice in order to maintain the cold as long as possible, and it would then be covered by the lid. Ice pails could also double as coolers for wine bottles when not being used for food.

As becomes clear, there was a great deal to a Georgian or Victorian dinner service, so the scope for collecting is vast. We should not forget either that the gentlemen had chamber pots hidden away in the sideboard for use after the ladies had retired from the table! These either matched the dinner service or were made of silver or pewter.

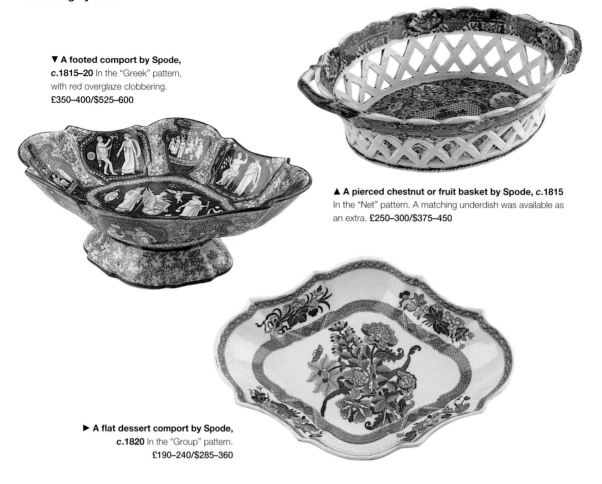

▼ **A footed comport by Spode,**
*c.*1815–20 In the "Greek" pattern,
with red overglaze clobbering.
£350–400/$525–600

▲ **A pierced chestnut or fruit basket by Spode,** *c.*1815
In the "Net" pattern. A matching underdish was available as
an extra. **£250–300/$375–450**

▶ **A flat dessert comport by Spode,**
*c.*1820 In the "Group" pattern.
£190–240/$285–360

# Dessertware

Dessert was also a very important part of the meal, and most of the great British factories produced dessertware just as they did dinnerware. As mentioned above, an ice pail would form the central feature of the table decoration. Ice was also used to make ice cream and sorbets, as well as to keep them cool. The shapes of items for the dessert service were always more decorative in style. In the centre of the table stood elegant footed comports, with an assortment of flat, shaped comports to match. There were also cream tureens, differing from the sauce tureens of the dinner service in that they often had a fixed base and were more of a boat shape. Ladles in the shape of sauce ladles, with pierced holes – known as sifter spoons – were used for serving thick cream while allowing the thin liquid to drain back into the tureen.

Fresh fruit was widely served; the very wealthy even grew their own pineapples – much smaller fruit than we know today. Pineapple stands were available (but they are very rare), and footed grape dishes rather like small cake stands were placed at regular intervals around the table, with a pair of grape scissors for diners to help themselves. Pierced baskets with a matching stand were used for soft fruit or crystallized chestnuts (as above). These were made in many designs and were naturally very fragile, being pierced or woven in construction. Some had holes in the base to allow excess juice to drain away.

Small dishes, either singly or in sets on a ceramic tray, were used for pickles or sweetmeats. Custard or syllabub cups – some with lids, some with handles, some with neither, and usually in sets on a footed stand – were used to serve fruit custards and other semi-solid desserts. There are some very interesting shapes to be found – it is quite possible to build up a collection of custard cups alone, which is an advantage if space is tight.

Dessert plates can be either pierced or arcaded – the difference being that in arcading the edge is formed by a looped, pierced, and arch-like

◄ **A pierced dessert plate by Spode,** *c.*1818–20
In the "Tower" pattern.
£150–190/$225–285

▲ **A rare fruit basket and under dish by Spode,** *c.*1820
In the "Italian" pattern. This is an unusual shape for Spode. £800–1,000/$1,200–1,500

▲ **A cup by Spode,** *c.*1820
In the "Italian" pattern – note the clobbering on the border. £100–120/$150–180

undulation, usually in a plain dark blue; while, in the case of pierced plates, the piercing puncuates the border pattern and doesn't affect the shape of the edge of the plate. A pierced plate may be incorrectly referred to as a ribbon plate (in the late Victorian period plates were often made so that decorative ribbon could be threaded through the holes). Some dessertware had gilded edges to distinguish it from the other tableware.

On small-sized dressers, dessert shapes usually fit in better in the narrowest spaces between the shelves. Because of the delicate and fragile design of dessert items, care should be taken when purchasing. These items all restore very well, so many repairs are very difficult to detect with the less experienced eye. Run a finger lightly around the edge to see if there is any change in the texture either on the face or the underside of the item, and look for any colour change. This is still arguably the most reliable way to check, though of course be wary of the seller too.

Clobbering is the term used to describe hand-painted embellishments on an item after the final glaze firing. This is not the same as gilding. It was often added to dessert items to give a lighter and more decorative feel to the object. Colours vary, but a crimson red was the most extensively used colour on blue printed pottery. This technique is an acquired taste, most collectors preferring the plain blue – though it does seem to be popular with the American market.

The "Greek" and "Etruscan" patterns made by Spode appear to be the designs most commonly decorated in this way. The "Greek" pattern can also be found clobbered in green or yellow. Care should be taken when purchasing clobbered items as the painted enamel lies on top of the glaze, unprotected and so liable to chipping. Collectors have been known to attempt deliberately to remove the enamel, but without success.

The "Beaded Frame" series and the "Drover" pattern, both by William Mason, have flowers in the border highlighted using pink, green, yellow, and brown. For some reason this seems to be more acceptable to collectors. In the end, of course, it is all a matter of personal taste.

▼ An egg cup stand by Spode, *c.*1825
In the "Filigree" pattern. It is unusual to find a
complete set with all the egg cups.
£650–750/$975–1,125

▲ **Central egg tureen from a supper set, by
Spode, *c.*1820** In the "Group" pattern. It would
originally have contained an egg cup stand.
**£350–400/$525–600 without internal stand
£700–1,100/$1,050–1,650 with stand**

# Supper & Breakfast

Supper and breakfast were the two least formal meals of the day, and the tableware for both meals was interchangeable. Breakfast usually consisted of vast meals of eggs, meat, offal, kedgeree, home-made bread, cheese, and preserves. Breakfast ale, usually home-brewed, was served to the men in small half-pint ceramic mugs, rather than glasses.

The size of the plates was smaller, usually 20cm (8in) rather than the normal 25.5cm (10in) dinner plates. The cooked meal was served on a large platter under a domed ceramic or silver cover, and the family helped themselves to the food as and when they pleased, as the meal was not at a set time like dinner.

Boiled eggs were very popular: special egg cruets were available with holes to hold a number of egg cups – anything from four to eight at a time. They sometimes had an oval salt cellar in the centre, and were made in several designs – round, oblong, or square, and with or without a handle. These stands *always* had matching egg cups and were not designed to hold the eggs directly; most eggs would

fall through the hole! Egg tureens were also available, usually as the centrepiece to a supper or breakfast set. They were made to contain hot water above which the eggs would be placed to keep warm. Some have a free-standing eggcup stand; others have a pierced plate for the cups, which fits inside; and some have an alternative shallow dish for use with scrambled eggs.

For supper, a light meal was prepared and left in a supper set for the family when they returned from the theatre or other function – the Victorians were wary of "night starvation" and felt they must eat before retiring to bed. These sets are either round or circular, and fit in a mahogany tray, usually with brass handles. The egg cruet or tureen tends to fit in the centre, and is usually surrounded by four shaped lidded dishes. Some of the earlier supper sets comprise many more small dishes, which all fit together snugly in the tray. All the segment dishes originally had lids; to find a complete set, especially in the original tray, is quite rare. Always inspect the tray

**▲ An egg cup stand by Minton, *c.*1830**
In the "Floral Vase" pattern; a more uncommon shape than the usual round or oval-type. This would stand alone, and was not part of a supper set. £550–650/$825–975

**▲ A lidded supper segment dish by Spode, *c.*1820**
In the "Greek" pattern; one of a set of four needed to make up the oval shape. £230–290/$345–435

very carefully for signs of wear and tear; there should be evidence of scratching both inside and out. Always inspect the corners of the dishes for signs of damage or repairs – these areas are especially vulnerable. Because of their slightly domed shape, the lids also are liable to have fine cracks both at the corners and at the centre under the handle. Spode, Minton, and Davenport produced a fair quantity of these sets, along with some other less well-known makers, though by no means did all factories make them. Many modern trays have also been made, which is quite acceptable as long as the buyer is made aware of their recent manufacture.

Individual dishes are more easily found, and with patience it is possible to make up a set . Because of their awkward shape, the lids are not always a perfect fit even on complete sets. Odd lids and bases can make an interesting and decorative display on a wall, although extra care is needed to ensure that the plate wires are secure and of the right size. A complete supper set can take up a great deal of space

# The "Greek" pattern

**▲ Detail of the border from the "Greek" pattern, by Spode** From the segment dish on the left.

Three main factories made this pattern. In Herculaneum's usually unmarked version the border comprises a "Greek key" pattern with six oval medallions containing classical figures, some with musical instruments. The central design of leaves is surrounded by an inner border of classical figures, including a team of horses pulling a chariot. The outer rim of the plates is often painted with an ochre enamel.

Spode introduced their extensive "Greek" tableware pattern around 1806, in response to the public's taste for classical themes. The source for the designs was *Outlines from the Figures and Compositions Upon the Greek, Roman, and Etruscan Vases of the Late Sir William Hamilton*, drawn and engraved by Thomas Kirk and published in 1805. The border remains the same throughout, showing four urns and four medallions with figures, and a central design which changes with the size of the object. A collection devoted to this design is an impressive sight, as there is so much detail, and the quality of both the engraving and the potting is superb. The design was continued throughout the Spode periods, though not so much in the Copeland era. It is still made today, but not with the same depth.

The third manufacturer was Wedgwood, at the Ferrybridge factory. This series was introduced before either of the other manufacturers' versions, and is known as the "Kirk" series after the engraver of the original designs. There is much more white on this design, and it does not appear so popular with collectors.

▲ **A complete "Greek" pattern supper set by Spode, c.1815** In a replacement mahogany tray. Very valuable when complete with the central egg cruet with matching salt cellar, and all lids. **£2,500–3,000/$3,750–4,500**

in a collection, so give some thought as to where it will be displayed. The top of a dresser or the pot board underneath is not always wide enough; always carry measurements and a tape measure.

Pickle, sweetmeats, and fruit cheeses also featured in the supper menu (although some considered cheese and fruit too heavy to sleep on), so single pickle dishes and sets were used. Pickle dishes come in a variety of shapes and sizes, some being very fragile leaf shapes, with a leaf vein pattern impressed into the pottery both inside and out. The tips to these dishes are especially vulnerable, chipping very easily – be aware of the edges as they are sometimes plain blue with no pattern, so may have been "touched up": always run a finger lightly around to check. Some pickle dishes are made loosely in the shape of a fish, the tail being the handle, which suggests that they could have been used for fish roe or something similar. Pickle sets come in a stand not unlike an egg cup stand, containing a set of shaped dishes with or without a handle, sometimes with a central salt cellar. As with supper sets, to find a complete pickle set is unusual. Some pickle dishes are of a

heavier nature, though they are still susceptible to damage, especially near the handle.

Patty pans, small circular or oval pans about 5cm (2in) across and 2.5cm (1in) deep, rather like a small pie dish, were used for meat pâté and fruit cheeses. Straight-sided small oval pots about 5cm (2in) across and 4cm (1½in) deep are potted meat dishes. They often have a small ridge at the top to enable the user to tie string around them, and no rim. Potted meat and fish were made by finely grinding meat or fish and mixing it with butter, then packing it firmly in the pot and sealing it with melted butter to preserve it – the Victorians hated waste. Patty pans and potted meat dishes are often stained from the high fat content of the ingredients, which permeated under the glaze. They can be cleaned professionally, but do not try yourself with any strong household cleaners.

Smaller supper sets, about 30.5cm (12in) in diameter and without lids, were made in the middle of the nineteenth century; these fitted onto a large plate and occasionally a mahogany tray, and were also used for hors d'oeuvres.

# Collecting
# Egg cups

▲ **An egg cup by Spode,
c.1820**
The "waisted" shape, in the
"Broseley" pattern.
£140–160/$210–240

▲ **An egg cup by Spode,
c.1818–20**
The "flared" shape, in the
uncommon "Japan" pattern.
£160–220/$240–330

▲ **An egg "hoop" by Spode, c.1830**
Using the border from the "British
Flowers" pattern. "Hoops" are double-
ended to take small or large eggs.
£70–110/$105–165

An egg cup collector is known as "pocillovist", and the field is "pocillovy" – long words to describe the collecting of such a small object!

Most of the blue printed egg cups that are available do not date before the early part of the nineteenth century. Earlier ones that do appear are usually in porcelain. They vary in size, shape, and design, but almost all would originally have belonged to a set that went with an egg cruet. The egg cups fit into the tray of the cruet, which stands on a plinth, and are usually plain white below the top. Those for the flatter type of stand are decorated on the foot too. In order to hang in the trays without falling straight through the holes, most have a narrow band at the top. These are referred to as "frame" shaped. Often they are decorated with only part of a border or the nankin, so the maker and pattern are difficult to determine.

Other shapes include the "antique" or "flared" shape, which fans out at the top and stands on a small pedestal base. This style seems to be more recognizably decorated and the maker's name is often on the base. The other fairly common shape is the "goblet", which is rather like a small wineglass; these are often thicker and so sturdier. The double-ended "hoop" is an unusual shape – either waisted or straight, and rather like a napkin ring (indeed, napkin ring collectors have been known to purchase these for their collections). The two ends may be different sizes in order to accommodate

varying sizes of eggs – such as a chicken egg in one end or a turkey or goose egg in the other (early nineteenth-century examples of these are unusual).

A greater quantity of these large double-ended egg cups were produced in the early twentieth century – particularly by Copeland, who made them in many patterns. Egg cups at this time were often attached to a base rather like a saucer, providing a space for the spoon; there are also double egg cups with an integral salt cellar. As they are small, egg cups take up little room, but as with any item collected with enthusiasm a collection can eventually take over. Unless a damaged egg cup is rare or part of a set it is not usually worth restoring it. Prices range from £20 ($30) to the low hundreds (no more than $230), depending on the rarity of the piece.

There is an egg cup society, the Egg Cup Collector's Club of Great Britain (www.eggcup-world.co.uk), which is open to international members. Founded in 1983, it provides a quarterly newsletter, and deals with the whole spectrum of egg cups available rather than focusing purely on blue-and-white printed versions. It is nevertheless very informative, and provides a forum for sharing the passion that many people have developed for collecting these objects.

▼ **A cup and saucer,**
*c.1820* In the "Bee
Catcher" pattern.
Maker unknown.
£190–240/$285–360

▲ **A part tea set in the "Goldfinch" pattern,**
*c.1825* The shape of the jug and sucrier suggest
a north-eastern pottery.
£900–1,200/$1,350–1,800

# Tea Wares

The drinking of tea was first introduced into Great Britain in 1700, and has continued to be an important aspect of the British way of life ever since. However, at that time coffee and chocolate were more widely consumed than tea. Owing to their rising popularity, coffee houses in London not only served the drink for consumption on the premises but also provided a take away service, so that customers could enjoy coffee at home.

Tea was first brought to England by the East India Company, at a very high cost, and was therefore only consumed by the wealthy classes. As tea needed to be kept dry on the voyage by ship from China, a non-perishable cargo that would not be damaged by sea water was required to provide ballast in the lower hold of the ship. The solution was to import fine underglaze-decorated porcelain: because the pattern was underglaze this was not affected by sea water. Vast quantities of tea items were imported to in England this way. Tea bowls were used in place of cups with handles as they were

less awkwardly shaped, making them easier to pack and fit into a tight space. Teapots, milk jugs, and basins were also imported.

Thus began the rapid growth of tea wares as we know them today. Eventually, in 1833, the East India Company lost the monopoly on the import of tea and the price fell, making tea available to almost everyone. Even most servants had an allowance for the purchase of tea and sugar included in their wages.

Most early English tea wares that were not imported from China were made in porcelain by the great British and European factories. The demand for matching, or at least "toning", tea services to go with other blue printed wares in the household prompted potters to manufacture them. Sets became available from most factories, and some patterns appear to be confined to tea items only. A typical set consisted of twelve cups and saucers, twelve coffee cans, a teapot with cover and stand, sugar box, slop basin, and a cream or milk jug. The saucers were used for both cups and

► **Coffee cans by Spode, c.1815–20**
In the "Lyre" (left) and "Vandyke" (right) patterns. The "Vandyke" includes gilding around the rim.
£140–220/ $210–330 each

◄ **A teapot by Wedgwood, c.1900**
In the "Peony" pattern. An "SYP" ("Simple Yet Perfect") design, with a sliding lid and feet to keep the pot on its side when the tea is brewing.
£200–250/300–375

cans, and were deeper than today, usually without a ring for the cup – possibly because the tea was drunk directly from the saucer, perhaps so that it would be cooler. Not all were won over by the pottery however, some families preferring to use a silver teapot and jug rather than ceramic ones.

Tea drinking was a great social event; it was quite acceptable for young people to attend tea with parents, this providing one of the few opportunities available at the time to meet visitors. The mistress of the house, or the eldest daughter under supervision, prepared the tea for the guests; the boiling water in a silver kettle delivered by the servants was kept warm on a burner, the mistress then mixed the tea after taking it from a locked tea caddy, and served it to her guests. It was served at four in the afternoon, or after dinner to the ladies who had retired to the drawing room. The men appeared much later, after consuming port and brandy in the dining room. To indicate to the servants that they had finished their tea, guets would lay the spoon across the top of the

cup. There was much competition between households with regard to who provided the finest tea, and possessed the most attractive tea wares!

Most of these items have become separated over time, especially cups and cans, so that few complete sets survive today. Breakages were frequent – particularly to the handles, which were so easily knocked on stone sinks.

The gradual introduction of luncheon in the 1840s, moving dinner to the evening so that there were only two main meals a day (a hearty breakfast and a late dinner), brought about the rapid growth of afternoon tea including bread and butter and cakes. The seventh Duke of Bedford's wife Anna is said to be the instigator of this fashionable habit that still survives today, since she could not endure the wait between meals.

Collections may concentrate on any or all of the items used in the consumption of tea or coffee. Coffee cans are popular because they are easy to display or can easily be fitted in between other items

▲ **A miniature tea kettle,**
***c*.1790–1800** In a
"Chinoiserie"-style pattern
**£450–700/$675–1,050**

◄ **A large and extremely rare tea kettle by Adams, *c*.1815**
In the "Seasons" pattern. The twisted rope handle was very lucky
to survive daily use. **£2,500–3,500/$3,750–5,250**

on a dresser. Many factories produced coffee cans, but few marked their wares. Attribution therefore relies on the pattern and any distinctive shape of handle. Take care when purchasing, as damage to the base of the handle is common, cracks occurring around this area. Perfect examples can be found except in the very rare patterns. There is often gilding to the rim and handle – again, watch for signs of wear. Cups should be checked in the same manner. Saucers are susceptible to hairline cracks because of their shape, so always view them in a good light. Special cup and saucer stands are available to display these pieces to their best advantage.

Teapots and coffee pots were made in a variety of shapes and sizes; the fashion of the time dictated the style, so they would often mirror the shapes used in silver, ranging from tall and slender to squat, and from rococo to plain. As with other objects, factories developed their own style, easily recognizable with experience. A teapot stand made to fit usually came with the teapot, though many of these did not survive or were used for other purposes. Collecting teapots requires space, and

can be expensive. Always buy in perfect condition if possible. Spout ends are vulnerable to damage, so test carefully for restoration with a finger, as well as at the base of the handle. A horizontal crack at the base of the handle is common, as this area seems to be a site of great weakness; also small hairline cracks often appear nearby. On the lid, check that the finial or knob is intact and not re-glued, and look for signs of a running of the glaze or different coloration, especially if the area is white in colour – white is one of the most difficult colours to match during restoration. There are often chips on the inside rim of the lid, which is only to be expected considering its use. Look inside the pot for signs of damage: some restorers do not restore the inside of hollow objects. Never try to clean the inside of a teapot with household cleaners. The spout may be full of old tea-leaves: to remove these allow the pot to soak in warm water to soften them, then gently flush them out from both ends – do not use a brush.

Novelty teapots, such as the "Simple Yet Perfect" example illustrated on the previous page,

## Identifying
## The "Love Chase" Story

▲ **A tea bowl and saucer by Spode, c.1820**
Showing the "Love Chase" pattern. £230–290/$345–435

▲ **A Spode teapot and stand, c.1830**
In the "Union Wreath" pattern. It is unusual to
find the matching stand with the teapot.
£390–450/$585–675

were popular but were not made until the
twentieth century. Made by Wedgwood, they are
an interesting addition to any collection, however,
as their odd shape has a practical purpose. With the
teapot upright on its base, tea-leaves are placed
in the pierced upper half of the pot, and boiling
water is poured into the chamber below. After the
lid has been replaced, the teapot is tilted backwards
onto its feet, allowing the tea to brew in the hot
water. When the tea is ready, the pot is placed
back on its base so that the tea-leaves and the
brewed tea are kept separate, so creating the
desired strength of tea.

Take note of the holes inside the teapot by the
spout: the very experienced eye can tell the possible
maker from the positioning of the piercing.
Ceramic tea kettles were used to hold the boiling
water before the mixing of the tea and are very rare.
Georgian and Victorian examples command high
prices and are greatly sought after. The two
illustrated here, both in perfect condition and of a
similar age, show the difference between the
normal size and miniature versions.

The "Love Chase" story tells the Greek
mythological tale of the renowned
huntress and athlete Atalanta, possibly the
daughter of Zeus (*ref.* Vol. 1 of Coysh's dictionary, *see* Further Reading, page 153). All of
Atalanta's suitors had to enter a race with her in
order to win her hand in marriage, the price of
losing being execution. Aphrodite, goddess
of love, gave one competitor, Milanion (or
Hippomenes), three golden apples. During the
race, Milanion dropped the apples one by one,
and each time Atalanta was so fascinated that
she stopped to pick them up, believing that she
would still have time to catch him up. Of course
this was not the case and Milanion was able to
win the race and take her hand in marriage.

The "Love Chase" pattern produced by
Spode, and later reproduced in the Copeland
period, depicts this tale. It is found mainly on
tea wares of beautiful quality in a medium to
dark blue, often with gilding applied to the
edges. It is very rare, turning up in specialist
sales or sales of whole collections, and not often
marked with the maker's name. The later
Copeland copy is quite common and much
thicker. A number of special limited editions
were produced in 1994, with an inscription on
the back, to commemorate the twenty-first
anniversary of Friends of Blue, the blue-and-
white collectors' club (*see* page 23).

▶ **A Spode cup and saucer, *c*.1830**
In the "Union Wreath" pattern.
£140–180/$210–270

▲ **A "Willow" pattern cow creamer, *c*.1850**
It is unusual to find one of these undamaged.
Maker unknown. £400–450/$600–675

▶ **A Spode tea bowl and creamer, *c*.1820**
In the rare "Turk" pattern.
Tea bowl £150–190/$225–285
Creamer £190–260/$285–390

Cream and milk jugs are interesting to collect, as the shapes and sizes vary not just from factory to factory, but also between patterns by the same maker. Creamers differ from milk jugs as they are usually oval in section, while the latter are round and slightly larger. Many of the cream jugs follow the traditional shapes found in silver. Though some creamers are quite small, holding enough for one person, they were usually of a similar design to the accompanying teapot or coffee pot, and were often available in more than one size. When checking for restoration, bear in mind the same points as for other tea wares.

An unusual design is the "cow creamer" illustrated here, which is decorated with the "Willow" pattern, though other rarer transfer printed examples are available. Be particularly careful when purchasing these items, as there are many reproductions around, and it can be difficult for the new collector to tell the difference. Pay attention to the ears, horns, and small lid, which are all vulnerable to damage. Restoration can be difficult to spot on items such as these, because the

ears and horns are usually hand-painted anyway, so the best advice is to buy from a reputable dealer.

Sugar boxes with lids did not have an aperture for the spoon, and seem large in comparison to the ones produced today. They usually take the shape of the teapot without the handle or spout. Typically, it is most unusual to find one today that has retained its lid. Both jugs and sugar boxes can be stained from use; it may be possible to have them cleaned professionally, but sugar can be very difficult, the dark molasses finding their way under the glaze.

Chocolate cups and pots should also be mentioned here. Chocolate cups are usually taller and slimmer than tea cups, with a flared top and sometimes a fitting lid. The saucers are smaller and have a recess to prevent the cup from slipping, with the sides coming up higher than a normal saucer. Complete examples are difficult to find. A chocolate pot is a smaller version of the coffee pot (both are taller and thinner than teapots) and they do not usually have a strainer at the base of the spout inside. Judging by the lack of examples found today, far

▲ **Detail from the border of a Spode teapot stand**
Note the rounded moulding around the edge of the stand,
which creates a more ornamental, even rococo, look.

▲ **A sugar box or sucrier**
**by Spode, *c*.1820**
In the rare "Milkmaid" pattern. About
10cm (4in) high. **£450–550/$675–825**

fewer were produced than teapots and coffee pots.

A very appropriate pattern to start a tea wares collection is the "Tea Party", made by Thomas Fell and other north-eastern potters, and found on teapots and jugs as well as cups and saucers. It shows a couple having tea in a garden with a servant in attendance. Another maker of this pattern is Scott, the Southwick Pottery, whose design, unlike the others, includes the figure of a begging dog on the right of the tea drinkers. William Smith & Co. made a similar version, with a different border. All these patterns can be found quite easily, but the quality of the printing and the potting varies from good to very poor. This is one pattern for which it is worth waiting for a good example.

With patience it is possible to make up a complete tea set in a single pattern, but collecting different patterns is arguably more interesting. Some designs seem to appear only on cups and saucers, perhaps originally to complement the family silver rather than have matching pots and jugs. Most years it is possible to find at least two new patterns on tea wares so keep hunting.

The term "gadrooned edge", or "gadrooning", is used to describe a raised, moulded edge, usually plain white, outside the border pattern. Spode introduced this style around 1825 on the "Jasmine", "Blue Rose", "Union Wreath" (I, II, and IV), and other similar floral-inspired patterns. Plates with gadrooned edging tend to be slightly larger in size. The Spode teapot illustrated (on page 107, and its stand above), is a good example of a gadrooned-edge teapot. Staining is particularly difficult to remove from Spode's "Union Wreath" gadrooned items, perhaps because the glaze is so white and possibly harder than for with other Spode patterns.

Other factories such as Hicks & Meigh used a similar edge on their ironstone china, but because of the composition of the clay this did not have the same translucent appearance as Spode's. Although the Spode gadrooned "Union Wreath" patterns appear very modern in design and shape, most date from the mid-1820s. Particular attention should be paid to the rim, as small chips can be difficult to detect: use the finger test.

Some collectors feel that items such as these do not fit into a general collection of transferware, but this is obviously a matter of personal choice.

◄ **A nursery bedpan by John Meir, *c*.1825**
From the "Byron's Views" series, showing the
Simplon Pass. £650–750/$975–1,125

► **A miniature tea set by Metheven, *c*.1850**
Showing the "Farm" pattern. It is unusual to find a
complete set. £350–450/$525–675

# Children's & Nursery Items

Victorian children were meant to be seen and not heard; in well-to-do households, children were presented to their parents washed, clean, and fed, for short periods perhaps twice a day. Most of their young lives were spent in the care of a nanny or nursery governess. Young babies might be taken to their mothers for feeding, but even this appears to be the exception rather than the rule.

The range of blue printed items made for the nursery was extensive. The first item required for a baby was an infant feeding bottle. Baby bottles hold a certain fascination for many people, and it can take quite a while to find examples. The best way to describe them is as being torpedo-shaped, with a tapered end for the baby to suck from and a central hole on the top for filling. Because of their awkward shape they were understandably almost impossible to clean properly – not surprisingly the infant mortality rate was extremely high at this time. Most of the bottles are basically the same shape; some are more bulbous, and the feeding tip may be raised,

though the most usual examples are flat. The quality of the transfer is not always perfect, as a special copper plate would not necessarily have been engraved for the object. Very few, with the exception of the various Spode partnerships, were marked with the maker's name. The "Tower" pattern by Spode most commonly appears on these bottles, but others are also found. Minton, Wedgwood, and Ridgway are among the other factories that made bottles. Infant feeding bottles were produced by moulding the two halves and then fixing them together, the joining ridge remaining visible around the sides of the bottle – this is a point where damage can occur, the seam being liable to separate. The feeding tip and the filling hole are other vulnerable areas.

There is a very attractive pattern of flowers and butterflies that can be found on bottles and other nusery or medically related items, though I have only found one very good quality piece marked Minton. The choice of feeding bottles

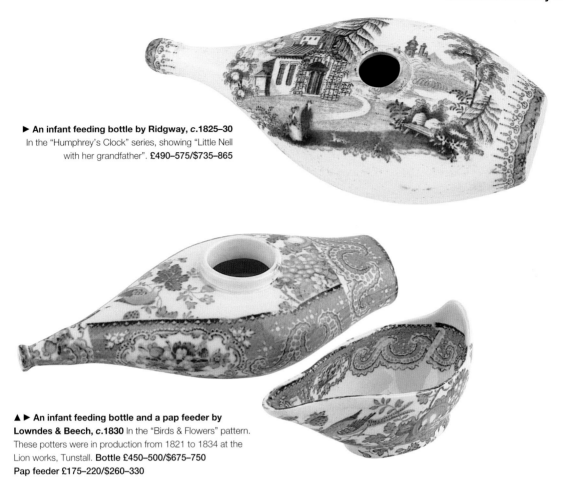

▶ **An infant feeding bottle by Ridgway, c.1825–30**
In the "Humphrey's Clock" series, showing "Little Nell
with her grandfather". **£490–575/$735–865**

▲ ▶ **An infant feeding bottle and a pap feeder by
Lowndes & Beech, c.1830** In the "Birds & Flowers" pattern.
These potters were in production from 1821 to 1834 at the
Lion works, Tunstall. **Bottle £450–500/$675–750**
**Pap feeder £175–220/$260–330**

is limited – if a damaged or restored one is available, the best advice is, if you like it, buy it.

Another item is a pap feeder, shaped like a small gravy boat but without the handle. These were produced by many factories, but few examples are marked. Pap was a mixture of flour and water, of very little nutritional value, that was fed to older babies and invalids using these specially designed feeders, rather than a spoon. Although flour was known to contain weevils (small beetle-like insects), the importance of infection control was not understood in the 1800s. Pap feeders were readily available at one time but are becoming scarcer now; they are popular with the Japanese, who reportedly use them for sauces. The likely areas of damage are the sides and the tip of the spout, where hairline cracks are often found, and they may be stained from use. Because of their size they do not require a lot of room to display, and when a small collection is placed together the wide variety of shapes is very noticeable. An interesting

pattern by Ridgway, made around 1840, is the "Humphrey's Clock" series, depicting scenes from Dickens's *Old Curiosity Shop*. This is printed in a pale blue, not to be confused with the later pattern printed in a dark blue and found on toy china from the early part of the twentieth century. The earlier pattern is often found on bottles, pap feeders, and other similar items, and is often marked "Humphrey's Clock". Sometimes only the border pattern appears on the smaller items.

Many bottles and pap feeders were printed using a sheet pattern, on which the joins in the transfer are quite visible. Some of these designs seem to appear only on bottles and pap feeders, possibly because of the odd shape of the items; it is possible to collect matching bottles and pap feeders. Both items are very popular with collectors who belong to the medical and nursing professions.

Small invalid feeding cups were also available for children. Sick children were cared for at home, where they were confined to bed for long periods, as

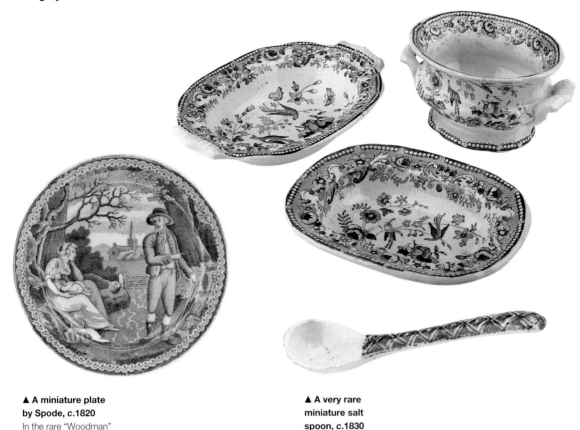

▲ A miniature plate
by Spode, *c.*1820
In the rare "Woodman"
pattern.
£180–200/$270–300

▲ A very rare
miniature salt
spoon, *c.*1830
In the "Willow" pattern.
£120–150/$180–225

bed rest seemed to be considered the only cure for many ills. The small nursery bedpan illustrated on page 110, with a total diameter of no more than 25.5cm (10in), is one of a very small number surviving. It is attractively decorated both inside and out, with a long hollow handle for disposal of the contents. Such pieces have been used to hold a central floral table decoration at dinner parties – an unusual recycling of such an object! Any other small-size toilet items that you may come across will have been made for the nursery, the majority having the same patterns as the normal size items – special nursery patterns were not as widely used as they are today.

Items for the nursery were thus usually simply smaller verions of the china used by the rest of the household, though plates with the alphabet or numbers around the edge were in common use. They might have a nursery rhyme, proverb, or motto in the centre. These objects were more likely to be used in the "schoolroom", where a governess was often employed by more than one family, with the children attending one house for schooling. Small mugs with similar decoration were also

available – a collection of alphabet mugs, each bearing only a single letter, would take time to build but would be very satisfying. Most of these pieces are transfer-printed in other colours as well as blue.

Individual plates and mugs with the name of a Sunday school and a religious inscription occasionally appear on the market. Children were not encouraged to play in the same way as they are today. Special toy, or doll's, tea or dinner sets were made for children to play with, under strict supervision and possibly only on special occasions. Spode produced a number of these, most frequently featuring the "Tower" pattern. Except in size, these miniature sets were identical to the originals in every way, including the ceramic ladles. Complete sets are rare today, but can be collected piecemeal.

Other factories produced toy items, one of the most extensive being the "Minton Miniatures" series introduced around 1825, which shows a variety of British views varying with the type of object being decorated. The name of the place is usually marked on the underside. Because of their nature and size, many have been lost or broken over

**◄ Davenport miniatures, c.1850**
Printed in green, in the "Birds & Flowers"
pattern. £40–70/$60–105 each

**▲ A plate by Clementson, c.1840**
Printed in purple. Made for the Wesleyan
Methodist Chapel Sunday School.

# Collecting
# *Miniatures*

**▲ Spode, c.1820**
A miniature cup & saucer in the "Daisy & Bead" pattern.
£140–190/$210–285

the years – sets handed down through families were perhaps not cared for as well as by their original owners – so their prices might seem excessive to the new collector. David Metheven, another manufacturer of miniatures, whose tea set is illustrated on page 110, was a Scottish potter from the Kirkcaldy Pottery in Fife from 1840 to 1861, when the factory was taken over by Andrew Young, retaining the name David Metheven & Sons until 1930.

The later version of Ridgway's "Humphrey's Clock" series, made at the end of the nineteenth and into the early twentieth century in the dark blue, proved popular. The title is stamped on the underside along with "England", and some of the later pieces also have the date of manufacture impressed. Many of the other Staffordshire potters made children's toy china. Often items were made in the same shape but decorated and marked by different potters – it is thought that factories sold the undecorated blank biscuit to others for decorating. Collecting toy china can prove an expensive hobby, and it particularly needs a safe area in which to be displayed, away from pets and (ironically) children.

Collecting china miniatures used to be the preserve of wealthy upper-class ladies. Minute in size and usually displayed in a cabinet or on a *bijouterie* table in the drawing room, these pieces were to be shown to and admired by friends and visitors to the house.

Miniatures are sometimes confused with the samples carried by the travelling salesmen for the china retailers. Miniatures, as the name suggests, are accurate copies of the larger items – exactly the same except on a miniature scale. Samples used by salesmen, by contrast, were made in the shape of the larger item, but usually only decorated in white. Accompanying the sample would have been a "trial" plate with samples of the new patterns available, and one example of a full printed pattern.

Miniatures, like toy china, were used by children, and so not surprisingly many have been lost and damaged over the years. Also, single items were given away, thus breaking up the set. Even today it is all too easy to lose a lid or spoon among packaging. Take great care to strap all lids together with the pieces they belong to and always pack everything in the same box; taking precautions at the beginning saves undue stress at a later date. Miniature vases and toilet items were also made, and some are particularly small. Take care with the insurance for a collection of miniatures: an apparently small amount can be of surprisingly high value when totted up. There are specialist books available on miniatures and toy china.

▶ **A vegetable tureen by Enoch Wood, *c.*1820**
Showing Lanercost Priory; note the wonderful lion finial.
£350–450/$525–6755

▼ **A soup tureen by Godwin, *c.*1820**
Showing "View of London & St Paul's".
£1,000–1,200/$1,500–1,800

▶ **A sauce tureen, cover, stand, and ladle, *c.*1815–20**
Showing Pashkov House, Moscow. It is unusual to find such an item complete with all its parts. **£390–450/$585–6755**

# Tureens

A tureen is basically a lidded receptacle for serving food or liquid at the table, rather than having meals served on plates. The largest of the tureens is the soup tureen, its size depending on the size of the family whose food it would contain. They were originally made with a matching undertray or stand, and all had lids with an aperture for the ladle, though not all had a ladle as these were available only as an optional extra, many families preferring to use a silver ladle. These tureens are by far the most decorative and impressive item in a dinner service. They provide a stunning centrepiece for the dresser, but check the size before you buy as some are very large. The ladles were matching, but you could aim to find one with a handle that matches in tone, as it will be the only part visible once in the tureen and it will still add to the display. Because of their size and the fact that they were used for hot soup many did not survive, and usually there were no more than two soup tureens per service. The undertrays either

have handles and a recess for the base of the tureen or are similar to a small-size platter. To confirm whether an undertray belongs to a tureen (and is not just a platter being used as an undertray), check the edge of the stand, which should be approximately parallel with the tip of the tureen handles, and in proportion to the rest of it. Large tureens may be stained from the fat content of the hot soup, which may have damaged the glaze on the inside. Always have them cleaned professionally.

Sauce tureens are usually the same shape as the corresponding soup tureen but much smaller, again with a stand and optional ceramic ladle. They were used for either hot savoury sauces or gravy, and there were usually a minimum of four per service – but this depended on whether gravy boats were used too. Dessert services had their own sauce tureens, used for cold sauces or cream, which had a fixed base (or stand) as an integral part. They are often boat-shaped, rather like a giant eye bath, mostly without handles, and the lids appear flatter

► **A vegetable tureen by Davenport,** *c.*1815–20
In the "Bamboo & Fence" pattern.
£250–300/$375–450

▼ **Spode cream or dessert tureen,** *c.*1815–20
In the "Greek" pattern. The base is fixed, and
there are no handles on this type of tureen.
£300–350/$450–525

▲ **A vegetable tureen by
Spode,** *c.*1815–20
From the "Caramanian" series.
£650–750/$975–1,125

than the savoury sauce tureen lids. Not all households had a separate dessert service, so dessert or cream tureens are more difficult to find. Some collections are devoted solely to sauce tureens, most insisting on having the complete set with the ladle.

The areas to which you should pay special attention when buying both soup and sauce tureens are the same for each because of the same basic shape. Around the hole in the lid for the ladle there may be fine hairline cracks visible only in a good light; look out for cracks around lid or tureen handles and chips to the rim or the base – all these can be restored, but the piece must then be sold as damaged or restored. The ladles are extremely vulnerable because of their thin shape; the most common area for damage is the base of the handle where it joins the bowl of the spoon. Watch for any change in the colour or texture of the pottery at this point, and check the bowl for hairline cracks. Ladles are very difficult and costly to restore, the restorer often having

to build a scaffolding structure around them in order to get a good repair.

By far the most common, and perhaps the least popular, tureen is the vegetable tureen. These are usually square or oblong in shape, although later ones may be round, and the lids are domed to allow room for the vegetables. Some have very decorative finials, such as the lion one illustrated, while some have a flat pierced draining plate, which fits into the bottom of the dish – as usual, however, it is very unusual to find one complete. Larger vegetable tureens sometimes had a straight-sided dish into which they fitted, which was filled with hot water to keep the food warm.

Another object that should be included here is a hash dish, which is a very large pie dish with a domed lid used for serving hash (cooked meat cut into small pieces and recooked, usually with potatoes). The bases are fairly common, but the domed lids are very rare. These items look stunning on the lower pot board of a dresser.

▲ **A drainer by Thomas Till, *c.*1840**
In the "Royal Cottage" pattern, thought to be the
Royal Lodge at Windsor Great Park.
£350–400/$525–600

# Drainers & Strainers

Drainers, or to give them their other name "mazarines", are oval pierced plates made to fit in the centre of a meat platter within the outer border. The purpose is twofold: first to allow the meat juices and fat to drain from a joint of meat or game, and second either to keep a whole fish flat to prevent it breaking or to drain the water that the fish was poached in. They were made to fit the largest two or three platters and used in place of a well-and-tree platter. The pattern matched that of the platter, usually without the border pattern, and depicted the same view. Not all dinner services had one, as they were only available as an optional extra.

To facilitate lifting there is a large central hole, the remainder of the plate being pierced with smaller holes, often in a pattern – on inspection of the underside, an interesting design formed by these holes may emerge, and it can be possible to deduce the maker from the design of this piercing. Many examples are marked, but the pattern name is often absent. Most factories produced drainers, and some also produced small draining plates to fit into vegetable tureens, though these are less common.

Because of their particular use, drainers are very susceptible to damage. Pay special attention to the area around the small holes for signs of chipping, as this can be difficult to see. Some drainers are made with small feet, while others have a rim to minimize contact with the well of the plate; both these areas are liable to damage. Make sure that the drainer sits well on a flat surface, and feel for signs of restoration. It is possible to find a platter with its matching drainer, but this need not be the goal by any means.

Drainers are easy to hang on a wall without the need for a wire plate hanger. Suspending them using a strong nylon thread through the holes with a safe knot is a good way of displaying them. A collection of drainers looks very attractive displayed high up just below ceiling level (after

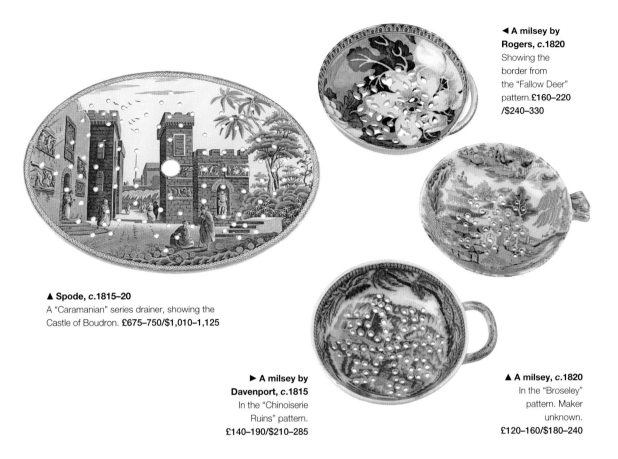

**◀ A milsey by Rogers, c.1820**
Showing the border from the "Fallow Deer" pattern. £160–220 /$240–330

**▲ Spode, c.1815–20**
A "Caramanian" series drainer, showing the Castle of Boudron. £675–750/$1,010–1,125

**▶ A milsey by Davenport, c.1815**
In the "Chinoiserie Ruins" pattern. £140–190/$210–285

**▲ A milsey, c.1820**
In the "Broseley" pattern. Maker unknown. £120–160/$180–240

ensuring that the fitting is secure!). Because of their holes they can also be displayed over a ventilator in a bathroom or kitchen without restricting the airflow. Drainers can be mixed and matched using different colours for an interesting collection. As with other items, prices can vary, starting low for a "Willow" pattern example and rising to the upper hundreds (up to $1,500) for a rare pattern.

Strainers come in a variety of shapes and sizes, and their original purpose is open to discussion. The three examples illustrated are thought to be "milseys" used for straining milk. Before the days of refrigeration, the most usual way to keep milk fresh was to boil it, then keep it in a jug in the larder. The skin that formed was unpalatable floating on top of the tea, so a milsey was used to strain the milk when pouring it into the cup. As may be imagined, these small objects measuring 5cm (2in) to 8cm (3in) in diameter were easily lost or damaged. There appear to be more in the earlier "Chinoiserie" patterns than anything else; whether

this was because they were less in demand after 1815 is not known. Strainers in the Spode, Minton, and Rogers patterns from around 1820 are known to exist, but very few others have been found. Shapes vary, having either one or two handles, whether "loop" or "flat" in form. Apart from the Spode examples, very few are marked. Unless the factory produced miniatures, a separate copper plate was unlikely to be engraved especially for a milsey because it was so small. It can sometimes be very difficult to decide which pattern is being used, and indeed to identify the maker.

Other items of a similar shape, some up to 10cm (4in) in diameter, were produced with purposes varying from lemon drainer to egg poacher or egg white strainer. Their specific uses will no doubt be a subject for discussion for a long time to come. Larger strainers, about 20cm (8in) in diameter, with small feet, were used for straining soft fruit or watercress, and originally had a plate underneath to catch the drips.

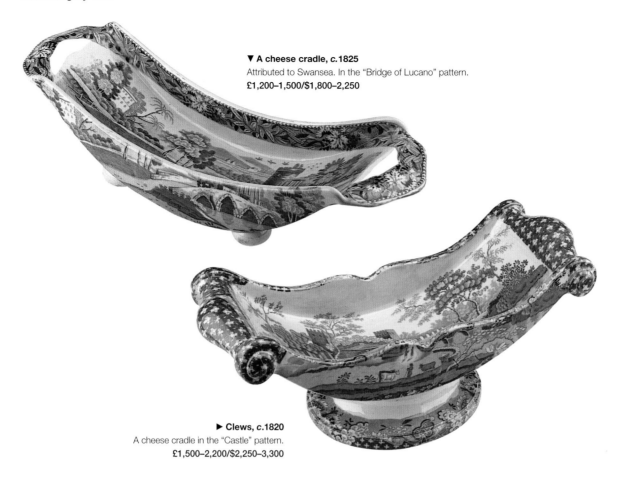

▼ **A cheese cradle, *c.*1825**
Attributed to Swansea. In the "Bridge of Lucano" pattern.
£1,200–1,500/$1,800–2,250

► **Clews, *c.*1820**
A cheese cradle in the "Castle" pattern.
£1,500–2,200/$2,250–3,300

# Cheese Dishes

Acheese dish, to most people, is a wedge-shaped dish in a tray, made to fit a classically shaped cut of cheese. However, this particular shape was not produced until the 1860s. Earlier dishes for serving cheese were wooden cheese cradles, usually in mahogany and sometimes with small casters to allow for movement around the table.

The popularity of cheese dates from the 1760s, when most of it was made on large estates, each with its own dairy parlour. The flavour of the cheese was dependent on location and the type of pasture on which the cattle grazed – producing a range of cheeses such as Cheshire, Gloucester, Wensleydale, and of course the world-famous Stilton. It is possible to visit the dairy parlours of some English stately homes, where all the equipment used in the making of cheese is displayed. This may include the very rare cream pans and milk pails, and of course a selection of cheese dishes. A cheese dish is still the best way to keep cheese fresh in a fridge without killing the flavour.

Wedgwood and Spode were the first potters to produce a ceramic dish specially for serving cheese. These were later referred to as cheese or cake stands, as they were also found useful for cake, though their main purpose remained the serving of cheese. All were footed and circular in shape, from 25cm (10in) to 36cm (14in) in diameter, the height varying depending on the factory. The original stands did not have a ceramic cover as it was thought that air was good for the cheese (perhaps this is not as illogical as it seems, as most cheese at the beginning of the nineteenth century was hard cheese). The Spode versions were available with a glass dome, which Spode was able to obtain as he sold bought-in glass along with his own ceramics from his retail outlet in London.

Spode first introduced cheese cradles around 1810–15: these were very similar in style to the original wooden cradles and proved to be popular. The whole circular cheese was placed on its side in the cradle and wedge-shaped pieces

◀ **A cheese dome, *c*.1880**
In the "Hawthornden" pattern. Maker unknown.
£250–350/$375–525

▶ **Copeland, *c*.1900**
A cheese dish in the "Italian" pattern.
£200–250/$300–375

were cut from the top. Considering this cutting method it is a wonder that any cradles have survived to the present day!

Stilton cheese originated in the Leicestershire area of the British Isles, and has a very pungent aroma. As Stilton became more popular, demand increased for a special Stilton cheese dish with a lid to contain the strong aroma. There are two distinct types of Stilton dish, the first being the Stilton pan. The Stilton pan is a shallow circular dish about 5cm (2in) to 8cm (3in) in height, often with small side handles, and a large high cover which fitted tightly onto the pan. The second, aptly known as a Stilton "bell", has a bell-shaped cover also fitting tightly into a raised groove on a flatter base. The Stilton bell is thought to have originated at the Bell Inn near Stilton, which is credited with introducing Stilton cheese to the general public. All Stilton dishes have a tight fitting lid to contain the smell of the cheese, but they all also have air holes at the top to allow the cheese to "breathe". The general design

of Stilton dishes remained very much the same until the middle of the nineteenth century, few being made because of the high level of skill needed in their firing; the production quality depended on the temperature in the original biscuit firing process. Many were lost either through cracking or breakages; they also took up a great deal of space in the kiln. The later dishes had a flatter base, and the lids were designed to fit less snugly, in order to allow a greater margin of error in the manufacture.

The wedge-shaped cheese dish, very similar to the ones used today, was first produced around 1860 in several sizes, and made to match dinner services. It was originally believed that non-Stilton cheeses should be open to the air, but as cheese became more popular it was discovered that part of the joy of eating cheese was the aroma particular to each type, and a cover was necessary to preserve this. However, as with Stilton dishes, all cheese dishes, whatever the shape, have at least one air hole, usually near the top handle, so that the cheese can

▲ **Spode, *c*.1820**
A very rare butter tub in
the "Blossom pattern".
**£600–750/$900–1,125**

► **A Stilton bell by Spode, *c*.1820**
A rare cheese bell in the "Italian" pattern. The
name "bell" is thought to originate from the Bell
Inn near Stilton (as well as being an apt name
for the shape). **£2,000–2,500/$3,000–3,750**

breathe. Some butter dishes were made to mimic
small cheese dishes, but you can distinguish these
from the latter as they do not have an air hole.

Because of these developments in the practice
of cheese eating, there are many interesting designs
to collect. The most commonly found item is the
cheese stand – many a collection has started
because someone has bought one of these for
practical use. Unlike other items, this one is very
likely to be used, even if only on special occasions –
at parties they can be used to serve anything and
provide a topic of conversation. An unrestored one
in good condition is best: if there are small chips on
the base the item can still be used, but if there is any
restoration it cannot. With any cheese items, watch
for staining, which is likely because of cheese's fatty
nature; and as it was stored for long periods in the
dishes the staining is often difficult or impossible to
remove. Always have it professionally cleaned.

Cheese cradles are fairly rare – dealers may only
find one or two a year – and so good restoration is
acceptable, especially if you like the item. The shape
of the cradles varies depending on the maker; the

Spode shape is particularly fine and thinly potted,
and is generally smaller in overall size than some of
the others – as may be seen if you compare the copy
of the original shape illustrated on page 41 with the
two illustrated in this section. Whatever the shape,
the four upper corners are very vulnerable, as is the
centre of each side where the cheese knife may have
caused damage. It is a lucky collector indeed who
finds a perfect example. A cheese cradle is one item
that benefits from being displayed alone on a table
or sideboard. It needs to have a plain background in
order to set off the beauty of the shape, and so as to
not lose itself in a sea of blue and white.

Stilton cheese pans are very rare (I have seen
only three in twenty years – one each by Spode,
Davenport, and Rogers); the bases turn up alone
and are often mistaken for tureen bases, and the
lids do appear also, but you are unlikely to find
the two together. Cylindrical in shape, with a top
and two side handles, and rather top heavy, they
are not particularly attractive.

The Stilton bell is a very fine item, the one
illustrated being part of my own collection – a rare

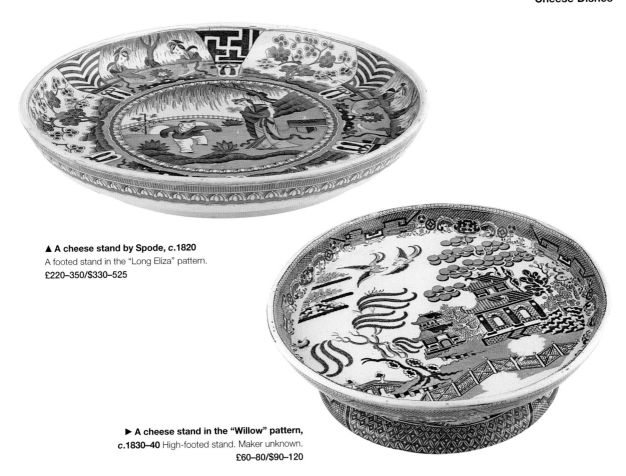

▲ **A cheese stand by Spode, c.1820**
A footed stand in the "Long Eliza" pattern.
£220–350/$330–525

▶ **A cheese stand in the "Willow" pattern,**
**c.1830–40** High-footed stand. Maker unknown.
£60–80/$90–120

and precious find. When originally bought, this object was extremely stained, taking several months to clean. Such items may also have a particularly unpleasant smell of rancid cheese, which can be dissipated by placing a raw onion inside. The base of this Stilton bell is heavy, having a large attached stand out of view underneath; it is marked "Spode" both in underglaze blue and impressed.

The later cheese domes have a flatter base, such as the "Hawthornden" pattern example illustrated on page 119. Their style is very similar to the Jasperware examples made by Wedgwood and other factories during the same period. The size may be a problem for display, but they look good on the lower pot board of a dresser or in a kitchen, and because of their younger age they are much cheaper than the early Stilton dishes, so would be more appropriate for practical use.

Wedge-shaped cheese dishes in many blue printed patterns became available after 1860 as part of the dinner service. Copeland made many in the "Italian" and "Tower" patterns, in more than one size, and still produce them in a similar

shape today. As individual manufacturers produced these in various sizes it is important, if you need a top to go with a base for example, to carry the measurements or a template with you when looking. Wedge-shaped cheese dishes are fairly narrow, so a collection devoted to them would fit on a slim shelf. As with cradles, to display the variety of shapes to advantage a plain background is better.

Butter tubs and dishes may be included in this section, since the later examples are often shaped like a cheese dish. The early nineteenth-century examples are usually round with a tight-fitting lid and are quite rare. The Spode example illustrated here is in the "Blossom" pattern, which is very rare itself. The later oblong butter dishes are large enough to hold a half-pound slab of butter, and usually have a ring or knob handle. As with cheese dishes the fat in the butter stains the base and sometimes the edge of the lid. Examples made in the twentieth century are less easy to clean than the earlier ones because of their harder, less permeable glaze.

▶ **A creamer by William Smith, *c.*1840**
In the "Bacchus" or "Lion Antique" pattern. £130–160/$195–240

▼ **A "Dutch" shape punch jug by Spode, *c.*1820**
In the rare pattern "Chinaman of Rank". £1,000–1,300/ $1,500–1,950

◀ **A puzzle jug, *c.*1820**
Attributed to Swansea because of its shape. In the "Thatched Cottage" pattern. £2,000–2,500/$3,000–3,750

# Jugs

Jug, pitcher, and ewer are all names for a handled receptacle to hold a liquid. In size these varied from miniature cream jugs to large one-gallon or more footbath jugs. Jugs are popular with collectors and impulse buyers alike.

The most unusual and fascinating jug must be the "puzzle" jug, which as the name implies is designed to puzzle the user. Of the several designs, the most common has a pierced top rim and a bulbous strip below, with three hollow knobs, each with a central hole. The handle is also hollow, and close inspection reveals a small hole on its underside. The trick is to pour the liquid from the jug without spilling it. This entails blocking some holes with fingers while allowing the water to pour from one – the method is a matter of trial and error! These jugs are both rare and unusual. Swansea appears to be the most prolific maker, though very few examples are marked and many are restored. Restored puzzle jugs cannot be guaranteed to work in the way they were originally intended to! However, they are

worth buying whatever their condition, as they are so scarce. The most common shape of jug is referred to by an original pattern book as the "Dutch" shape and exists in many sizes from the capacity to hold a few ounces to over a gallon. They were used for milk, or the larger ones for punch, cider, or ale. Most factories made them available in a set of graduated sizes. The smaller cream jugs, holding a quarter to half a pint of liquid, are of a more oval shape, very useful for filling gaps in a display.

Take care when looking for damage, especially in the base – hairline star-shaped cracks, however fine, will usually leak. Before using a jug, particularly if it is for flowers, fill it with water and put a piece of tissue paper underneath on a plate or mat, to test that it neither leaks nor is porous before risking it on a piece of furniture. Restored jugs are for decoration only, as over a period of time the restoration would start to lift off from contact with water. One option is to line such a jug with a cut-down plastic bottle that does not show over the rim.

▶ **A large lidded punch jug,**
**c.1820** Showing a version of
the "Village Church"
pattern. Maker unknown.
**£1,800–2,400/$2,700–3,600**

▲ **Minton, c.1840**
A "Blue Marble" pattern water
jug for a small washstand.
**£90–140/$135–210**

◀ **A water jug by Challioner, c.1840**
The name "Union" is printed on the underside.
**£170–230/$255–345**

The large slender or helmet-shape jugs are usually originally from a toilet set; the tall ones in particular are very useful for fresh or dried flowers. Toilet jugs, as they are collectively called, may come in more than one size in the same pattern, depending on the size of washstand for which they were intended. The very large jugs, usually with a second front handle, which was essential for lifting and balancing, were intended for use with a footbath. They are heavy when empty and so become almost unmanageably so with a gallon of water inside. The handles should be treated with care – never lift a jug by its handle, as you may be left holding only the handle. Watch for signs of restoration and damage on the spout, handles, and top and bottom rims – these are the most vulnerable areas. As with other large items, space is necessary for a good display, and they look more impressive on their own.

Another category is jugs with lids. Any jug that has a pierced strainer in the spout should have a matching lid. The size of these varies, the smaller pint-sized ones are usually hot milk or "toast water" jugs. Toast jugs were used in caring for the sick: burnt toast was placed in the bottom of the jug and boiling water added; the cooled liquid was then strained and given to the patient as a "medecine" believed to calm the stomach through the effect of the charcoal from the burnt toast. The larger lidded jugs, some holding in excess of a gallon, were usually for punch. Some of the very large lidded jugs were also used as harvest jugs, for carrying ale or cider to workers in the fields. This may seem extravagant today, but blue transferware was very cheap when produced and in everyday use, and ale and cider, often made on the farm, was a part of the workers' wages. Some harvest jugs, sometimes reffered to as bell jugs, had a loop handle going over the top, but these are difficult to find as the handle is so vulnerable. They also had a front handle to assist in pouring. There are more jug collectors than specific blue-and-white collectors, and several excellent books about jugs in general are available.

◀ **A pickle dish by Hicks & Meigh, *c*.1830** In the "Exotic Birds" pattern. £150–190/$225–285

▼ **A complete pickle set by Minton, *c*.1820** In the "Dove" pattern. £450–550/$675–825

▲ **A pickle dish by Spode, *c*.1820** In the "Group" pattern. £170–225/$255–340

# Pickle Dishes

A pickle dish, as the name implies, was generally used for serving pickles: not pickles as we understand the term today, but rather sweetmeats and spices. The most typical shape is that of a leaf, with jagged edges, the stalk providing the handle, and with the underside often moulded to resemble the veins of a leaf. Most of the great pottery factories produced these. There are also some of a similar shape but heavier, without the fine edges, and no veins on the underside. Some have a loop handle, others a small projection as a handle. Not all examples are marked with the maker's name, and because of their small size some are decorated with only part of a pattern or just a border pattern.

Very early pickle dishes, such as those made by Leeds Pottery, can be plain with a dark blue feather-type edge to them, and appear in some fascinating shapes not often found in blue printed wares. They make an interesting addition to a collection.

Some of the dishes are made in the shape of a rounded fish, and were possibly used to serve roe or other fish-based food. These tend to be slightly larger and made after 1830. As with other small objects, many have been lost or damaged over the years.

The "Group" pattern pickle dish by Spode, illustrated here, displays yet another shape, having small feet on the underside moulded in the shape of a spiral shell, again suggesting the use of these dishes for fish products. Spode made this particular shape in a variety of patterns. As regards damage, the area near the handle is very vulnerable to cracks and the underside chips easily. Some of the pickle dishes have gilding to the edges, which means it is possible that they were used in a dessert service, as gilding was popular for such items.

Pickle dishes came in sets of four or more to a dinner service. They were shaped dishes which often fitted into a larger dish forming a tray. Some of these have a small round or divided oval dish for salt or spices. To find a complete set is unusual, and to find one containing all the pieces in perfect condition is even more so. The small individual

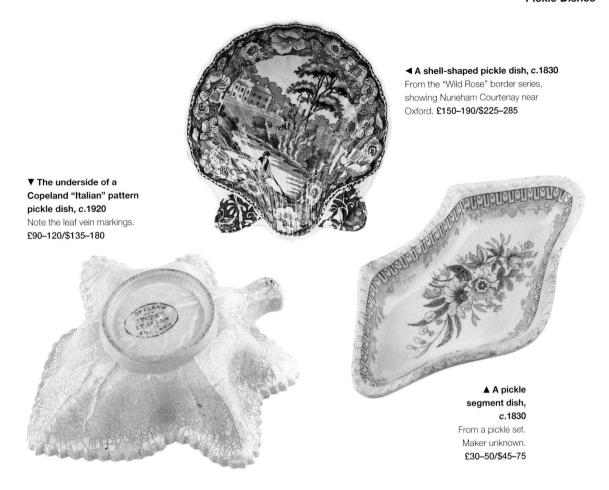

**◄ A shell-shaped pickle dish, *c.*1830**
From the "Wild Rose" border series, showing Nuneham Courtenay near Oxford. **£150–190/$225–285**

**▼ The underside of a Copeland "Italian" pattern pickle dish, *c.*1920**
Note the leaf vein markings.
**£90–120/$135–180**

**▲ A pickle segment dish, *c.*1830**
From a pickle set. Maker unknown.
**£30–50/$45–75**

segment dishes do turn up and are worth collecting: eventually you may put together a set, although some of these flat sets can be large, containing more than four dishes. Until you have seen a complete one, it is easy to mistake the bases for a flat dessert comport.

Footed pickle sets, like the Minton "Dove" pattern example illustrated, can be found with or without the central handle. Often in place of the handle there is a fixed salt cellar, sometimes in the shape of an open flower. These sets are very delicate, especially the corners of the segment dishes. It is always worth buying an incomplete set, as it may be possible to complete it over a period of time. Always carry a card template of the piece that is missing, as even things like this were made in different sizes.

Pickle dishes continued to be produced from the end of the eighteenth century up until the 1930s, the Copeland "Italian" versions probably being the most recent examples. Displaying pickle dishes may present a problem, because of their shape and the fact that most of them are decorated only on the inside: they are best viewed from above or on stands on their sides. Either way, they need to be in a safe place away from possible hazards. Although small in size their value soon mounts up, so be careful with the insurance and keep receipts for proof of value.

As can be seen from the illustrations on these pages, there are many different shapes and designs to be collected in pickle dishes alone. For example, one collector has over a thousand (not all of blue-and-white), amassed over twenty years, and is still able to find new examples to add to it. Because there are so many variations in shape it can be too easy to assume an object is a pickle dish when it may in fact not be – there is, for example, some debate as to the purpose of some small oblong dishes with a small handle at each end. These could be pickle dishes, spoon rests, or indeed the base for a small tureen – perhaps from a child's toy service.

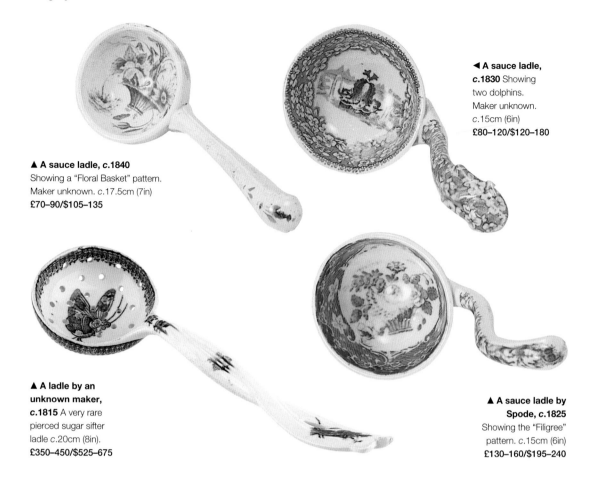

▲ **A sauce ladle, c.1840**
Showing a "Floral Basket" pattern.
Maker unknown. c.17.5cm (7in)
**£70–90/$105–135**

◄ **A sauce ladle,
c.1830** Showing
two dolphins.
Maker unknown.
c.15cm (6in)
**£80–120/$120–180**

▲ **A ladle by an
unknown maker,
c.1815** A very rare
pierced sugar sifter
ladle c.20cm (8in).
**£350–450/$525–675**

▲ **A sauce ladle by
Spode, c.1825**
Showing the "Filigree"
pattern. c.15cm (6in)
**£130–160/$195–240**

# Spoons & Ladles

Ceramic spoons are a rarity; because of their purpose and the construction of the handle, few apart from ladles survived. Ceramic caddy spoons the same shape and size as the silver ones are particularly rare, and small salt and mustard spoons equally so. A pottery salt spoon, found many years ago, is illustrated in this book (*see* page 112).

Ladles were made in three basic sizes, the largest for the soup tureen, the small for the sauce or cream tureen, and the very tiny for toy or miniature tureens. The toy or miniature ladles are the most difficult to find, being easily lost. They came in two sizes – one for the soup and one for the sauce tureen – and some are no more than 4cm (1½in) long. These are very expensive in proportion to their size, compared to the standard larger ones.

The sauce or cream ladles are all about 17cm (11in) to 20cm (8in) in length, and the diameter of the bowl is about 4cm (1½in) to 5cm (2in). The shape of the handle is very indicative of the maker, varying from straight to a sharp curve at the end. Very straight handles are usually Spode, but there are exceptions to this.

Decoration often just takes the form of part of a pattern or a border, making attribution difficult. Few, except Spode and some others, are marked. When you see a collection of many ladles together you become aware of the amazing number of variations in shape and style, and indeed in quality. An area to inspect for damage is the handle, especially at the base – lightly run a finger around this part to feel for any change in texture caused by restoration, also look out for any obvious change in colour. Very old restoration tends to turn yellow after a time, and the thin film of the new glaze may start to peel – a tell-tale sign. Another place to check is the point at which the bowl of the spoon joins the handle; any sign of separation here should be viewed with caution, as they can be liable to part when washed. Signs of wear on the underside of the bowl are to be expected owing to the constant contact of the spoon with the base of serving dishes

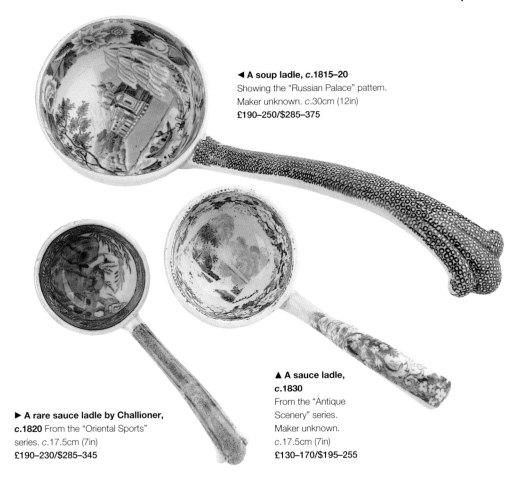

◀ **A soup ladle,** *c.*1815–20
Showing the "Russian Palace" pattern.
Maker unknown. *c.*30cm (12in)
£190–250/$285–375

▲ **A sauce ladle,**
*c.*1830
From the "Antique
Scenery" series.
Maker unknown.
*c.*17.5cm (7in)
£130–170/$195–255

▶ **A rare sauce ladle by Challioner,**
*c.*1820 From the "Oriental Sports"
series. *c.*17.5cm (7in)
£190–230/$285–345

and plates when ladling food from one to the other. Look out for thin hairline cracks, which are not always easily seen in a poor light; again, touch is the best way to detect damage.

Small ladles matching the sauce ladles, but with very small holes pierced into the bowl, are available but rare. These are called sifter ladles, and were used as part of a dessert service, either for serving sugar or for thick cream, allowing the thin watery whey to remain in the serving tureen. They have a very balanced feel about them; the handles are sometimes flatter than the conventional ladle. As we know, however, a matching ladle was not produced for every tureen, as many households preferred to use the family silver version.

Soup ladles are the same basic shape as sauce ladles but larger in size, reaching anything up to 36cm (14in) in length, with a bowl of 7.5cm (3in) to 10cm (4in) in diameter. They have the same weakness points as all ladles, and the long elegant handles are extremely vulnerable – great care

should always be taken when packing them. Patterns on these are usually more recognizable, as a transfer for a small plate may be used for the bowl of the ladle. The handles of ladles (and any other pottery item) may be decorated with a sheet pattern used solely for this purpose and common to several factories; and the undersides of some ladles are also decorated, creating a more interesting display. Display is an important consideration, aided by specialist acrylic stands designed to hold the ladle in a safe position; some ladles lie on their sides, others do not. Collectors have been known to hang them on a wall using a fine fishing line thread, but this is not recommended, as in order to hide the knots in the thread you have to cut the ends very close to them, making it more likely that they will slip undone (unlike drainers, where the knots can be hidden behind the item). A flat display case is another option. As ever, as long as the objects are secure, display is very much a matter of individual preference.

► **A bird feeder by Samuel Alcock, *c.*1830** In the "Ferns" pattern. This is a very rare bird feeder or "whistle", used in the cages of exotic birds.
£700–800/$1,050–1,200

► **An inkwell by Deakin & Bailey, *c.*1840** Showing the "Exotic Birds" pattern. Inkwells are rare.
£450–500/$675–750

► **An asparagus server by Spode, *c.*1790–1800** In the "Temple" pattern.
£170–240/$255–360

# Unusual Objects

Some objects do not fit easily into traditional categories such as dinnerware or toilet items. As we have seen, almost every kind of object was produced in blue printed pottery – there were few other mediums available other than glass, silver, and pewter, and none of the modern plastics that we are used to. Think of any item in everyday use and it was most probably made in pottery – blue printed pottery, more specifically, as the cobalt blue pigment was the first to stand up to the high temperatures in the kiln, and transfer printing being the most cost-effective means of decoration.

One of the more common of the unusual items is the asparagus server, used to divide asparagus into individual portions, to be lifted onto the diner's plate using either silver tongs or a silver slice. These were brought to the table on a large circular plate, holding the number required for the number of guests sitting at table. Accompanying this was a butter boat (illustrated on page 131), a very small item of about 2.5cm (1in) to 4cm (1in) in

length. This contained the melted butter with which to dress the asparagus. Few of these servers survive, as so many were damaged by the hot butter and lost because of their small size. Spode made the earliest butter boats, and "Chinoiserie" patterns can be found dating from around 1800. The shape of the handle varies from a simple wedge to an intricate loop or twig shape. Some have a straight side, while some curve outwards from the base; nones take up much space.

Inkwells are very rare: this is one object it is certainly advisable to buy even if damaged, as long as it is at a reasonable price. They come as a single object or as part of a desk set including other pieces of writing equipment, such as a pen tray and a sander to dry the ink, all of which are also rare – you may come across only half a dozen in the space of twenty years, none perfect. The wells are usually stained from the ink, of course, and the only way of combating this is to soak them in cold water, changing it regularly. A sander looks rather like a

▲ **A pair of window props by Ridgway,** *c.*1835 In the "Windsor Festoon" pattern. Originally part of a set of four, used to prop open sash windows. £550–750/$825–1,125

◄ **An Argyle,** *c.*1790
In a version of the "Temple Landscape" pattern. Argyles were invented by the Duke of Argyle in the late 1700s to keep gravy warm. £550–650/$825–975

pepper pot but with a flatter top. Some unscrupulous dealers may try to sell the base of a toilet box as a pen tray, so it is important to remember that pen trays were usually part of an inkstand and so had a recess for the inkwell, unlike toilet boxes.

The small bird feeder illustrated is only about 10cm (4in) in height. Sometimes referred to as a bird whistle, it was also available in a much larger size. In keeping with the taste for new experiences from far-away lands, exotic birds, kept in cages, were very popular in the Georgian and Victorian periods. However, bird feeders of any size are very rare and seldom seen. Dog and cat bowls could be included here, but they are much easier to find. They were presumably produced in larger numbers, as the more traditional domestic animals maintained their appeal in competition with more exotic creatures: certainly it is possible to find one or two a year.

Furniture lifters, such as those illustrated overleaf, are extremely rare; many were damaged,

not suprisingly considering their lowly (literally) funtion. They were used to protect the feet of furniture from damp on the stone floors, or to protect expensive carpets from damage from furniture. Either way, a life under heavy furniture carries a high risk of damage. As may be seen, two of the lifters have a flat side, so that the furniture could be placed flush with a wall. Window props (such as those above) are another very uncommon item, with a similar function to furniture lifters, being used to prop the lower part of a sash window to provide ventilation. As may be imagined many were lost after simply falling out of the window on to the ground. A complete set of four is very unusual. Some were made to resemble Staffordshire figures of Punch, though blue printed examples of this are yet to be seen by this author. As with furniture lifters, some damage must be expected.

A "veilleuse", used to keep broth, gruel, or tea, warm at night, is a two-handled cylindrical object with a small night-light, or "godet", in the base,

►▼ **A set of four furniture lifters by J. Holland,** *c.***1852–4** In the "Carra" pattern. Used to lift furniture off a damp floor, or protect the carpet from the furniture. £800–1,000/$1,200–1,500 set

which heats either a small bowl or a teapot. It is very unusual to find all the components together, especially the night-light, which is about 2.5cm (1in) in diameter with a separate lid with a small pierced hole for the wick, which floats in oil. These were kept burning at the bedside of invalids. Many are damaged, often with a cracked cylinder.

Flasks of any shape are rare. These are either round or oval with flattened sides, some having a central hole created with the aim of making them more portable, while others have small lugs at the side through which a leather thong or cord could be threaded in order to carry it round the neck. These are sometimes referred to as "pilgrim flasks". There is some debate as to the usual contents of these bottles, with suggestions ranging from water to wine or gin. They are almost impossible to clean as the neck is very narrow, being only a finger's width. Damage usually occurs on the neck or the top rim, and as they were moulded in two halves the outer edge is liable to split.

An "Argyle" is so called after the Duke of Argyle, who designed the first one, made in silver in the middle of the eighteenth century. This object resembles a small teapot, with either a flat or a domed lid. Its purpose was to keep gravy warm, achieved by giving the body of the object a double skin, and putting a central funnel inside to fill with boiling water. The spout runs from the bottom of the body and is usually narrower and longer than that of a teapot. Found by a collector almost by accident, the Argyle illustrated here (page 129) was first thought to be a fairly uninteresting teapot, but was then delightedly discovered to be a very rare Argyle. It has also since been passed over as simply being a "Chinoiserie" pattern teapot with a chip on the lid. This all demonstrates the importance of always checking items carefully, inside and out!

Toothbrush head covers, which were presumably used when travelling, are known to have been produced in transferware. They are small oblong containers of the appropriate size to fit a toothbrush head, one end of which has a slit for the handle while the other has a hinged lid totally enclosing the brush. The lid rim and hinge are made of lead. Since they are so small, it is little won-

▲ **A rare pilgrim flask,**
**c.1820**
Showing a floral border
pattern. **£500–650/$750–975**

▲ **A butter boat by Spode, c.1820**
Using the border from the "Italian"
pattern. Used for melted butter.
**£140–190/$210–285**

▲ **A chocolate cup saucer, c.1825**
By the Don Pottery, from the "Named Italian Views" series'
border pattern. **£170–230/$255–345**

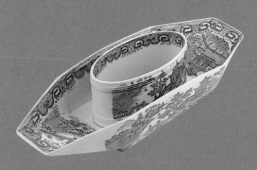

▲ **An asparagus butter dish by Spode, c.1820**
In the "Flying Pennant" pattern. Note that the lid is missing.
**£350–450/$525–675**

der that so few are found. Hinged soap boxes to match, though often damaged, are easier to find. They are most likely to be found in a "Willow"-type pattern, probably dating from around the middle of the nineteenth century.

A new shape whose purpose is not obvious has been found recently: an oblong box 15cm (6in) by 5cm (2in) by 10cm (4in) high, with a central division and a tight fitting lid, standing on four small square feet, and in the "Floral Basket" pattern. It could be a tea caddy by either Minton or Bathwell and Goodfellow, dating from around 1825.

Pipe rests are very unusual objects. Again, it is worth taking time to consider an item such as this – a fleeting inspection tends to lead to the mistaken assumption that it must be part of a larger object. They are small and boat-shaped, about 7.5cm (3in) to 10cm (4in) long, with a section cut out of one end to take the stem of a pipe, while keeping the pipe bowl upright. When one first encounters an object like this it can be very puzzling – but this element of the unknown, of finding unfamiliar things, is of course half the fun of collecting.

There is always room for debate as to whether an item or set is complete. For instance, a jug with a strainer in the spout should have a lid even if the inner rim is decorated (without a lid there would be a risk of the liquid flowing above the strainer). The long toilet boxes decorated on the inside also had lids. Vegetable tureens had lids unless they had a flat rim similar to a pie dish, in which case they were in fact open bakers. Always look for a recess for the lid; think about why the object is made the way it is. The saucer above is unusual – it is not obvious that the cut-out is where the handle of the tall chocolate cup would fit. The central dish of the asparagus butter dish is fixed to the base, but again it is not complete – it should have a tight-fitting lid with a handle. When a dish or bowl is undecorated on the inside, remember that it should probably have a lid; if it was meant to be seen it would have been made more pleasing to the eye.

▲ **A footbath by Spode, c.1815–20**
Of the straight-sided variety, in the "Tower" pattern.
£1,800–2,200/$2,700–3,300

◀ **A lidded waste pail by John Meir, c.1835** In the "Laconia" pattern. £750–850/$1,125–1,275

# Toiletware & Medical Items

Households of the late eighteenth and early nineteenth centuries did not have the fully plumbed bathrooms that we take for granted today. All ablutions were carried out in the bedroom. Each bedroom had a washstand, the quality of the piece of furniture and the decoration of the pottery depending on the wealth of the house. The servants had painted pine furniture and plain white pottery or enamel toilet sets. A full toilet set consisted of a jug and bowl, slop pail, chamber pot, footbath and jug, soap dish, brush pot or vase, and sometimes a bidet in a stand. Some washstands were double-sized to hold two pottery sets.

The brush or toilet boxes are fine items to collect, about 17.5cm (7in) in length and about 5cm (2in) wide, with a tight-fitting lid sometimes with a handle. The inside is often decorated, and has either a central division running lengthways, or two small ridges running crossways to keep the brush or razor dry. These dishes are very attractive and come in a wide variety of patterns. Sometimes they are

accompanied by a matching lidded soap dish, either round or square with a matching fitted pierced drainer to prevent the soap from sitting in water. Many of these have been separated from their lids or drainers, so a complete one is a good find.

It should be remembered that the servants brought all the hot water upstairs from the kitchens. It was carried in metal cans and transferred to the ceramic jugs in the bedrooms. The servants would also remove the slops placed in the ceramic pails or large lidded pots – life was very hard for chambermaids at the time!

Toilet sets were produced in vast quantities by most of the great factories; it is not always possible to find a complete set today but with patience you can match one over a period of time. The jugs and bowls were made in various sizes; Minton, using the "Genevese" pattern from 1830 well into the twentieth century, possibly made the greatest variety of sizes in jugs and bowls in a single pattern. Sizes ranged from the small bowl of about 23cm

◄ **A small washstand, *c.*1810**
In Georgian oak, containing a small jug and bowl by Rogers, in the "Flora" pattern (along with a small odd white soap pot, *c.*1830, maker unknown). **Jug & bowl £450–550/$675–825**

▼ **A bidet by Spode, *c.*1815–20**
A "Tower" pattern pan, in original mahogany frame, with replacement finial to lid. **£1,550–2,000/$2,325**

(9in) for the small washstand similar to the one illustrated, up to about 38cm (15in) in diameter. The jugs are all very squat in this pattern, their size always in proportion to their corresponding bowl. If buying them as a set always check that the mark is the same on both the jug and the bowl in order to make sure they were made at the same time – another way to do this is to make sure the colours match, as there can be great variations in the blue of items made at different times.

If trying to find a bowl to fit into an existing washstand, always carry the exact measurements or, better still, a cut-out of the hole – never try to guess the size, as you may end up dealing in wash bowls. Some washstands, especially the small square or corner units, have other smaller holes in the top apart from that for the bowl. There are usually one or two of these, for soap and a brush. The soap was in the form of a small ball and rather soft, made by the servants from wool fat (the natural lanolin extracted from the fleece of sheep),

sometimes with rose water or petals to perfume it. The soap dishes designed to fit these holes are straight-sided with a lip to prevent them from falling through. The smallest is about 5cm (2in) in depth and the larger brush pot anything up to 15cm (6in). As has been noted, however, it is quite unusual to find a complete set to fit all the holes; a near match is often the best you can aim for. Alternatively, a very small miniature soup plate will serve the purpose of covering an empty hole. If a toilet set is decorated with a serial pattern it is quite likely that the central patterns will differ on each item, with the borders matching, so remember that this does not necessarily indicate a matched set.

Some washstands have a small recess on a lower shelf to take the jug, which arguably looks much nicer than having the jug sitting inside the bowl, allowing you to see the whole object. The accompanying slop pail may vary in shape according to the maker. It might be a traditional pail shape with a wicker handle, with a drop-in lid forming a funnel

▶ **A vomit pot by Bovey Tracey pottery, *c*.1840** Showing the "Arched Bridge" pattern. **£220–290/$330–435**

◀ **A bourdaloue by Minton, *c*.1840** From the "Lace Border" series. **£450–550/$675–825**

down which the slops would be poured, or it could be a large covered receptacle with a tight-fitting lid and two ceramic side handles. Some of the lids are domed, making a very attractive shape that can be used in any setting – they look very good in a bathroom or bedroom, and are useful for storage or as a waste bin. Lidded pails have been described as many different objects, from wine coolers to bread bins. Because they were made by many factories the patterns are not always of a bedroom nature.

A footbath is a highly sought-after item, especially if in perfect condition. These were used originally not just for washing but for medicinal foot soaks such as mustard baths. The earliest ones are possibly Wedgwood creamware in plain white; most of the other potters made them around by 1815. Footbaths come in two basic shapes, the earliest being straight-sided, with raised bands on the outside, and usually with loop handles for carrying. The later shape, made around 1825, is more bulbous, known as "bombe". Most have a border decoration on the inside; some have all-over decoration on the inside or just on the inside base.

Even the same potter, using the same pattern, made footbaths in several sizes. Spode made at least three sizes in the very popular "Tower" pattern. As may be imagined, they were very heavy when full of water, so it is no wonder that the handles often suffered damage. Matching the footbath would be a large jug with a second small front handle to help in manoeuvring it when full. The great majority of these have some damage; to find a perfect example is quite an achievement.

Because of a life spent on the floor, many footbaths have suffered some damage: cracks, loss of a handle, or chips. They are popular as plant holders or for cut flowers, in which case it is advisable to line the inside with a plastic bowl in a neutral colour to protect the base from the effects of limescale or soil from the plant pots. A certain amount of restoration is acceptable on an item of this size, providing that it is sold as a restored item rather than claimed to be perfect. Always examine an item very carefully for signs of restoration or damage, and get a detailed receipt. A footbath blends with most decors, placed

◄ **A male urinal by Clyde Pottery, c.1840**
In the "Ravena" pattern.
£500–650/$750–975

▼ **A very rare eye bath or cup by Spode, c.1825**
In the "Willow" pattern.
£1,500–2,200/$2,250–3,300

◄ **A female urinal by Clyde pottery, c.1840** Also in the "Ravena" pattern – note the difference in shape between the male and female urinals.
£550–650/$825–975

either on the floor or on a table, or indeed up high.

The bidet is not a recent invention: the Chinese were producing them in the eighteenth century and British potters made them from about 1815–20. They were available with or without a matching wooden stool, the shape of which varied, the most common being oblong with a lid that dropped over the seat and ceramic pan to provide a table when not in use. The more unusual are made in the shape of the pan, with a drop-in lid. Some bidets have a plug hole at one end so that they could be drained into the slop pail or chamber pot, rather than removing the pan from the frame. The pans varied greatly in size, some factories producing more than one size in each pattern, such as Spode's "Tower". The pans were either decorated on the inside only or on the exterior as well. It is presumed that the totally decorated ones were for use on top of another piece of furniture.

A very rare item is the leg bath, shaped rather like a very large boot, with space enough to place both feet in together, allowing the water to come to just below the knee. The leg bath illustrated (*see* page 137) is by Minton, and another of the few existing is in the Spode Museum at Stoke-on-Trent. As may clearly be seen, the handles (one on each side) protrude so much that they are very vulnerable to damage or even total loss. This is one object it would be a good idea to buy even if broken, so long as most of it could be restored. Amazingly, this leg bath had suffered only minor damage having been used by the previous owner's children as a holder for tennis rackets and hockey sticks for the entire duration of their time at school.

It should be remembered that the majority of sick people were cared for at home, often employing the services of a nurse, and all babies were born at home. It was only the very poor or homeless who were cared for in a public hospital or workhouse until the latter part of the nineteenth century. Consequently the home sickroom was well equipped for the care of the patient at home. Chamber pots matched the toilet sets, and were available in various sizes all the way down to toy miniatures. Some chamber pots had a matching lid and a few had two handles, becoming known as

► A slipper bedpan by Copeland, *c.*1890
With a floral sprig decoration. £230–300/$345–450

▼ Fixed top funnel-shape spitoon, *c.*1820
By Spode, in the "Tower" pattern.
£390–470/$585–705

▲ An invalid feeder by
Spode, *c.*1830
In the "British Flowers" pattern.
£225–290/$340–435

"marriage pots". There is much debate as to the use of the very small chamber pots, especially those with rounded tops rather than a flat rim. Small pots with a flat rim, such as the smaller of the two illustrated here in the "Italian" pattern, were probably used by children, a suggestion supported by the fact that they can inserted into a slot in the back of a child's chair. The small pots with a rounded rim are in fact more likely to be vomit or spitting pots, though this issue is still open to conjecture. Male and female urinals (*see* page 135 to observe the distinction between the two) were used in bed, as well as the small triangular slipper pan, which was used by female invalids – these are about 23cm (9in) by 10cm (4in), with a spout for emptying at one end, and are difficult to find. The "bourdaloue" is a boat-shaped receptacle rather similar to a large sauceboat, for discreet use by ladies under their long dresses and undergarments when travelling.

The introduction of the early pottery flushing water closet is credited to Wedgwood, who made creamware examples as early as 1777, the earliest blue printed examples being made by Twyford in 1809. The ceramic pan would be held in a cast iron container and be decorated with romantic-style landscapes. Examples do appear but many are damaged, and they are very difficult to plumb into a modern system. By the middle of the nineteenth century a flushing lavatory was considered an essential item in prosperous households. They are very much the same shape as the ones we know today and, providing that the pipe work is un-damaged, can successfully be put to practical use. There are some very atttractive blue printed ones to be found, particularly from specialist salvage dealers, who will be able to advise as to the fitting of them. As plumbing became more advanced the fitted washbasin, similar to that illustrated on page 145, became widely available. Many designs were used on these, most commonly the "Tower" pattern by Spode (and continued into the Copeland period), and they were available in several sizes. Again, these can be used today, but avoid harsh cleaners that may damage the glaze.

The incidence of chest disease around this time was very high – not surprsingly since smoking,

◀ **A leg or gout bath by Minton, *c*.1830**
In the "Chinese Marine" pattern. These items
are extremely rare. **£5,000–8,000/$7,500–12,000
depending on pattern**

▼ **Two chamber pots by Spode, *c*.1820**
In the "Italian" pattern. Child and adult
versions. **Adult £250–350/$375–525
Child £350–450/$525–675**

along with the chewing of tobacco, was a popular pastime. Most people, men in particular, had a productive cough – in response to which inns and hostelries tended to have a communal floor or table spittoon; members of the upper and middle classes also carried their own individual ones. These are available in a variety of shapes and sizes; all are lidded, some with fixed lids, and all have a spout for emptying. Another design is in the shape of a handled mug, with a separate funnel-shaped top; interestingly the inside of the mug is undecorated, even though mugs usually have at least a border of decoration inside at the top.

Invalid feeders are rather like a small teapot with a half-covered top, and either a side or back handle. These enabled the patient to take fluids when lying in bed and were made by most of the factories, in several sizes. Areas susceptible to damage are the tip of the spout and the half cover, as well as the base of the handle. A small collection of these will demonstrate the variation in shapes available; a matching pap feeder was also usually produced. Warming plates – a double-skinned

plate, with a spout through which you could fill the sides with hot water to keep the food warm – were also used in feeding, originally for invalids who were slow to eat. Some also have a small loop handle in order to hang the object to drain the water. Very rarely, it is possible to find the original ceramic stopper on a small chain that was used to plug the hole. Many of these suffered cracks, especially in the well of the plate or on the spout.

The eye cup or eye bath is a very rare and sought-after item commanding high prices, particularly when in perfect condition. Like many items, these were so small that many were lost, so it would be advisable to buy even a damaged one if you are lucky enough to find an example. Other items of a medical nature to be found include leech jars, chemists' jars, and ointment pots. This field is understandably widely collected by members of the medical and allied professions.

# Other Colours

## Take a break from the classic blue and appreciate familiar patterns from a new angle

◄ **A treacle jar printed in green, *c*.1840** Screw-top lid. Maker unknown. £350–400/$525–600

▲ **Soup tureen, lid, and undertray by Copeland, *c*.1890** In the "Field Sports" pattern. £350–450/$525–675

## Green

Green transferware was first produced at the end of the 1820s. Before this, blue was the only colour that remained stable in the kiln. Unlike the blue pigment, which is more of a black colour until after the final glaze firing, the green ink begins as green and remains unchanged from the application of the colour to the copperplate until the finished article is removed from the glaze oven.

One of the first green printed designs, and some say the best, was the "Aesop's Fables" series made by Spode around 1830 and continued well into the Copeland and Garrett period. Spode produced other notable patterns in green such as "Botanical", "British Flowers", "Floral", and "English Sprays", which were all well received by the buying public, who by then were growing tired of the blue. The range of items was far more limited, however, than for blue wares; most of the green output was confined to table and toilet items. On the other hand, green was not a popular colour with collectors until the closing years of the twentieth century,

but has since gained in popularity. In fact, the "Byron's Views" series introduced by Copeland and Garrett around 1835 is more sought after in green than in blue, even though (or perhaps because) fewer green versions were produced.

The shade of green varies according to the maker and the pattern, ranging from a grass green with a tint of yellow to the dark green of the "Camilla" pattern lidded broth bowl illustrated here. Any new design introduced after 1840 was of a romantic or stylized nature because of the constraints of the Acts of Copyright, which prevented the copying of known engravings. This led to less detailed designs and the depiction of nondescript castles and houses with exotic-sounding names. European-type locations featured heavily, but the scenes were wholly unrecognizable. Many patterns showing mountains and chalet-type buildings included "Rhine" in their name, but could in fact have been anywhere.

Davenport made the "Rural Scenery" series in

▶ **Copeland, *c*.1920**
A "Camilla" pattern lidded broth bowl
and saucer. *£45–50/$65–75*

▼ **A drainer by
Spode, *c*.1830** In the
"Floral Sprays" pattern.
*£350–400/$525–600*

◀ **A lidded toast water jug, *c*.1840**
In the "Asiatic Plants" pattern. Attributed to Minton.
*£170–220/$255–330*

green, showing typically romanticized country landscapes that could be anywhere in the British Isles as they are so unspecific. Various potters produced "Abbey Ruins", but which abbey no one knows. Minton produced many of their floral-influenced patterns in green, especially the dessert items, "Arabesque" being a particularly fine example. Some of the miniatures were also made in green but only in small quantities. Thomas Godwin's pattern "William Penn's Treaty" was more common in green than in blue, as it was produced for the American market, where this colour was popular at the time.

The screw-topped treacle jar illustrated here in a very dark bluish green is probably the darkest green produced. The fact that it has a screw mechanism makes it very interesting, as not many of these were produced. Each lid was made with the jar, and usually the same number is impressed into the lid and jar at the time of manufacture; the lid is very tight-fitting so presumably will only fit

its own corresponding jar. Treacle seeped through the glaze, so many examples are discoloured and very difficult to clean. When the lid is removed they often release a very strong smell – a cut lemon sealed in the jar should remove this. The toast water jug illustrated here in the "Asiatic Plants" pattern is a fairly common design found in green as well as blue.

The "Field Sports" series made by the Copeland factory at the end of the nineteenth century and during the early twentieth century was a popular design that may have only been made in green, showing various country pastimes such as hunting (the meets, full cry, the kill), and horseracing. As it is a serial pattern a different subject is shown on each size. It seems to appear only on tableware; the soup tureen illustrated is an impressive shape.

There are now many more collectors of green transferware than ever before. Whether it should be mixed with blue is a matter of personal choice.

▲ **A jug printed in pink, *c.*1830**
With the "Feeding the Turkeys" pattern.
Maker unknown. **£250–300/$375–450**

▲ **Small jug by Swansea,
*c.*1835** Printed with
acanthus and other
floral decoration.
**£190–220/$285–330**

◀ **Jug, by an unknown maker, *c.*1850**
Decorated in a sheet chintz design.
**£150–190/$225–285**

# Puce, Mauve, & Pink

Puce was one of the first experiments in using a colour other than blue. Some of the earlier pieces were not very successful: the overglaze, which starts with a blueish tinge, remained blue, and some of the pattern was more blue than puce – the plate by Deakin and Bailey illustrated here is a good example of an unsuccessful production, with an uneven colour. During the early 1830s the colour was perfected, but it appears not to have enjoyed the popularity of the other colours, as little is available today. Most of the puce was for export to America, so more is available there.

In 1835, Thomas Mayer produced the "Canova" pattern in puce, which was popular on tea wares, and his "Mogul Scenery" series showing stylized Eastern scenes with elephants proved popular on dinnerware. Minton produced some of their floral patterns in puce, especially dessert items and some toilet wares. Ridgway also made some, mostly with the stylized Alpine scenes, but few examples appear in Britain. John Wedge Wood, the great copier who

tried to adopt the Wedgwood name, made a small quantity of tea wares in puce.

The natural successor to puce was purple or mauve, found more on children's china and miniatures until around 1880 when it was mass-produced by many factories. William Adams produced both puce and purple, especially in the "Columbus" series depicting the adventures of Christopher Columbus. Some were decorated in more than one colour, using say both puce and green – as underglaze rather than one in clobbering.

By far the most popular of these colours was dark pink or red, made initially for export to the United States. As with the other colours, William Adams produced many patterns in pink or red. Most were of the romantic style typical of the patterns of the time, including the "Beehive", the "Chess Players", "Columbus", and "Fountain Scenery". Most of these designs cover the whole surface of the object, with little white showing. An extensive series by Adams printed mainly in red is

◄ **A cheese plate by Deakin & Bailey, c.1830**
Demonstrating an early stage in the transition from
blue to puce. £70–90/$105–135

► **Cork & Edge, c.1850**
A miniature plate printed in mauve,
with the "Fishers" pattern. £30–40/$45–60

"The Sea", showing various nautical views, including one of pirates. Another Adams serial design
shows the four "Seasons", also printed in blue,
green, brown, and black. The jug illustrated, by an
unknown maker, showing "Feeding the Turkeys"
in a picturesque farm setting, also depicts "skeps" or
beehives. This jug is now owned by a beekeeper
who collects anything bee-related – demonstrating
that you can theme your collection around topics
that hold a personal interest.

Ralph Hall made a series of designs in pink
showing "Italian Buildings", "French Châteaux",
and "Views in Sardinia", which are all stylized serial designs. Jackson made a quantity of red and pink
transferware, such as the "Antelope" on tea wares,
and the extensive "Clyde scenery" series on dinnerware, showing scenes in the Clyde area of Scotland,
including castles and country houses. A very
impressive series with some interesting shapes, it is
rarely found in Britain as most was made for export
to America. Another pattern not often seen in

Britain is "Harvest Scenery", by an unknown
maker. A very appealing pattern, it shows farmers
gathering in the harvest, with a plough, bales of
straw, and horses.

The "Napoleon Battles" series by Charles James
Mason, showing battle scenes, will appeal to collectors of military subjects. It was printed in blue,
green, and brown as well as pink. Anthony Shaw's
"Texian Campaign" series is another notable serial
pattern showing battle scenes. Ridgway made the
extensive "Pomerania" series of European landscapes in pink, as well as some floral patterns. The
Rogers factory produced a limited number of the
"English Views" series, but mostly for export.

The Spode partnerships did not start to use red
colours until the end of the nineteenth century,
when the Copeland family owned the factory.
Their two most common patterns are "Pink
Tower" and "Pink Camilla", both made in vast
quantities. Pink and red transferware, in particular,
is a rapidly growing area of collecting.

▼ **A children's, or miniature, plate, c.1840** Printed in black, showing the "Equestrian" pattern. Maker unknown. £50–60/$75–90

▲ **A platter by Edward & George Phillips,** **c.1830** Printed in brown, showing Eton College, Berkshire. £200–250/$300–375

▶ **A 20cm (8in) plate by Spode, c.1830** From the "Aesops Fable's" series, showing "The Dog & the Sheep". Printed in black. £140–160/$210–240

# Brown, Black, & Orange

Finally, the least popular colours with collectors seem to be the browns, black, and orange. The first recorded pattern transfer printed in brown was the "Water Lily" by Wedgwood in 1808 for a special order, though the colour was not generally well received by the buying public. Its popularity did increase, but this seems to have been dictated by fashion at the time. From a very rich dark chocolate brown to a pale almost sepia colour, the variety of shades exceeds the range of blues.

Apart from the "Greek" pattern very little brown was made by the Spode partnerships. Clews, Stevenson, and Jackson made several series of American historical interest for the American export markets. The Ridgway partnerships made a number of patterns, including "Pomerania", "Oriental Birds", and some of the floral designs. They also made the "Giraffe" pattern, which included a backstamp bearing the inscription "Published August 30 1836 Agreeably to the Act", the exact meaning of which is uncertain.

Charles James Mason produced the "Napoleon" series in three colours, but arguably the brown is the most impressive. The series includes "Battle of Austerlitz", "Battle of Marengo", "Napoleon's Battles", "Return from Elba", and "Revolt of Cairo". All were made between 1835 and 1845 and are uncommon in England, being principally for the export markets. Thomas Mayer made the "Abbey", "Canova", and "Olympic Games" patterns in brown, in addition to other colours. The Minton factory does not appear to have produced much in the way of brown, unless it was all exported. The "Texian Campaign" by Anthony Shaw and the "William Penn Treaty" by Thomas Godwin are in fact more common in brown than in other colours. Herculaneum, of Liverpool, made the "Archery" pattern in brown, and Edward and George Phillips made the "Eton College" platter illustrated here, and may have also produced other patterns.

A lot of children's toy and miniature items were printed in brown, even the "Minton Miniatures"

▶ **A plate by Spode,** *c.*1830
In the "Blue Rose" pattern. Printed in orange;
a very unusual piece. £80–120/$120–180

▼ **A soup plate by Spode,** *c.*1830
From the "Aesop's Fables" series, showing
"The Lion in Love". Printed in black.
£160–190/$240–285

▶ **A children's, or
miniature, plate,**
*c.***1840** Showing
"The Spotted Pig".
Printed in brown.
Maker unknown.
£50–70/$75–105

series. There is a very attractive miniature service dating from around 1840, available only in brown, showing "British Birds". Some unusual shapes make up the set, each having a different bird printed on it, and though the potting is very heavy, the quality of the print is good. Reportedly, "brown is the new blue" in America, though it is hard to say whether this trend will last or take off in Britain.

Black is a very stylish colour and is gaining popularity, especially with the interior design market, blending well with the new classical patterns and motifs used on wallpaper. Spode produced several of their patterns in black, which was in fact almost a dark grey. The "Caramanian" series is occasionally found in black, usually only on table items, and the "Aesop's Fables" series, as illustrated here on a soup plate, is available – though examples are more likely to be from the Spode, as opposed to the Copeland and Garrett, period. Ralph Stevenson made the "British Palaces" series in black, an extensive serial pattern showing a different view on each item, with

a backstamp that includes either the name "Lace Border" or "British Palaces". Each attractive scene, Windsor Castle in Berkshire and the Brighton Pavilion being well-known examples, is famed in a cartouche surrounded by sprays and small fleurs-de-lis. Bear in mind that the quality of black printed items varies to the extremes – the definition of some is quite striking if well potted, though the more mass-produced black can look very hard and uninteresting. Children's plates are often printed in black with a verse or motto, then hand-decorated with enamel in bright colours.

Orange is almost another variant of brown, and indeed some orange items may be failed efforts to produce brown. Spode made the "Blue Rose" pattern in orange, but this seems to have been unpopular as very few examples are available. The "Blue Rose" plate illustrated here is one of the very few early examples of orange that exist; most of what is available was made at the end of the nineteenth and early twentieth centuries.

# Display

◄ **A dresser rack showing assorted items of blue printed pottery, *c*.1800–30** Dressers are the classic method of displaying a collection. It is essential to make sure that something like this is fixed securely to the wall.

Display is such a personal matter, and depends on various factors – for instance, have you formed a collection with a space in mind? Was the collection or the piece of furniture inherited? A dresser (or hutch) is the first thing we think of to display a collection of plates, but even large items of this nature will not hold a vast amount. The space between the shelves is a major factor to be considered; on some of the very early dressers there is less than 15cm (6in) between the base and the first shelf and less than 20cm (8in) between the first and second shelf. Most dressers will take only three to four large platters on the top shelf; some have a lower shelf under the drawers known as a pot board, which is very useful for displaying large items such as a foot bath or a well-and-tree platter laid flat. Remember that children and animals can be very inquisitive and accidents do happen; always make sure that a dresser rack is secured to the wall, or you could risk losing almost all your collection when objects tumble at the slightest touch, breaking not only the

things on the rack but also any objects that might be below. Although most dressers have hooks for jugs or cups, be very wary of hanging antique pottery by the handle, as joins are always a weak point. Wall-mounted shelves are another option, but they are only as good as the fixings holding them to the wall.

Some collectors have purpose-built shelving and display cabinets made to fit a particular space, but this is restrictive if you later decide you want to move it to another room. Unlike finely decorated porcelain, blue printed pottery looks more attractive not behind glass, but on open shelves, in a more natural setting. The very small delicate items, however, are better off behind glass for their own protection. Always be aware of the danger that a collection can start to look like a museum display and take over the whole house. A plate shelf, high up at the level of a picture rail, provides a good safe display area away from the possible perils of visitors handling a piece. The only disadvantage of this is that being able to handle the pottery and get a feel

**▲ An antique wash basin, c.1840, and tiles, c.1850**
In use in a cloakroom. The basin is in the "Panorama" pattern and the tiles are by Minton. **Basin £450–550/$675–825 Tiles £40–70/$60–105 each**

for it is one of the joys of collecting. There are also self-adhesive discs with small hanging rings available to stick on the back of plates, though these are liable to detach from the plate eventually and also tend to cover the all-important maker's mark, so wire plate hangers are more advisable (*see right*).

On any restored items it is a good idea to attach a small label on a part that is not visible, to remind you that it is restored. Restoration is now so good that it can easily be missed at a later date and washed in water that is too hot.

The hand basin illustrated here, which is the same size as those used in boats, is in everyday use in a cloakroom. The original fitting was carefully removed and replaced with a modern waste pipe and plug and modern taps. Something like this is a source of much delight to visitors; the only drawback being the lack of an overflow pipe.

As with any aspect of collecting, only the individual can decide what works for them. A word of caution, though – do not have a large display visible from a window or door, on view to potential thieves, as individual pieces may not be that expensive but together their value soon adds up. Insure the items on your home insurance and keep a photographic record with the receipt. It is all too easy to forget some of the items, especially after a burglary. Use an invisible marker to mark items with the postcode.

# Using wire plate hangers

**▲ An old plate wire**
Rusty wires can cut into the plate, causing damage.

**▼ A plate wire correctly applied**
Modern rubber-coated wires provide far more protection.

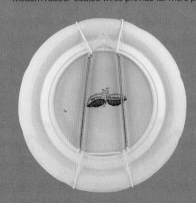

Wire plate hangers are a very good way to display plates safely on a wall, but only if the wire is of the correct size and the wall fixing is secure. Most modern wires are coated in a white or dark brown plastic to protect the edge of the plate from damage that used to be caused by rusty wire cutting into it. For added protection, a small piece of something like blu-tack under the wire helps. The springs on the plate wires can be supported by threading them through a fine wire, to prevent the spring stretching too far with the weight of the plate. Platters can also be safely hung the same way, using a specially produced large-size plate wire. Care must be taken when removing old rusty wires, which were often made to fit the individual plate. Never attempt to bend the wire, but try instead to slide a piece of fabric under the wire and gently cut or saw the wire to remove it, cleaning the plate afterwards. Always work on a non-slippery surface.

# Labels

It is important to be aware of the significance of the small labels on the back of pottery, and remember that they should never be removed. These labels often provide valuable information as to provenance, and indicate previous owners of the piece in its life as a collector's item. The labels on the plate illustrated here show that it was originally part of the Little collection – William Little being the author of *Staffordshire Blue*, the first book devoted to collecting blue-and-white pottery (*see* Further Reading, page 153); and that it was later sold to the McCarthy collection, owned by a pioneering female surgeon, from whom it and many others passed into this author's hands. Finally it is now in the Robinson collection, the number on the label being a reference number for this collection. The other label bears the price and description from a sale many years ago. Labels such as these provide an interesting and detailed history of an item; some of the specialist auctions of a single owner sale have a label to that effect. Keep *all* the labels on.

Items over one hundred years old are exempt from value added tax and import duties to America; to take full advantage of this a certificate of age is necessary. Certain other countries such, as Canada, Australia, and New Zealand, also require certification of age before an antique is imported without duty. The label that can be seen on the under side of the pickle dish here shows that it passed the necessary inspection and gained a guarantee of its age, stating that it is "certified to be over one hundred years old" and stamped "British Antique Dealers Association 1937". After 1939 the label was altered to say "Certified for customs purposes only". These labels were supposed to have been removed by customs at the point of exit from England, but not all were, which not surprisingly lead to misuse as the labels were taken off to use on uncertified goods. This practice was stopped in 1967, when it was made a requirement for a certificate to be issued along with the goods after they had been inspected, and a reference number used on the back instead of the label certifying age.

Other interesting labels can also be found – such as those bearing a price, often in the old pre-decimal coinage of pound, shillings, and pence. The often very low price can show what a good investment blue printed pottery was and still is. When an item is sold through an auction house, a coded seller

**▲ Collectors' labels**
The selection of labels on the reverse of this plate indicate its provenance since it was sold by the original owner, creating a picture of its history.

**▲ Certificate of age**
A label applied by the British Antique Dealers Association verifying the age for export purposes.

identification label will be attached to it so that the auctioneer knows the owner of each piece being put up for sale, while the buyer has no way of finding out their identity. Some collectors prefer to dispose of their surplus items this way as it is completely anonymous. These are the only labels that can be removed as they serve no further purpose.

# Care & Repair

▲ **Damage to the glaze of a platter by frost**
Similar damage may also occur if household bleach is used
for cleaning pottery. This platter shows the "Village Church"
pattern, c.1825 £50–70/$75–105

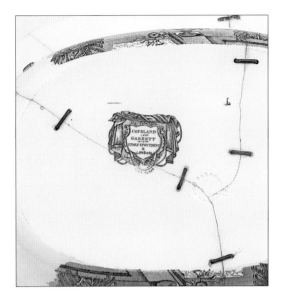

▲ **Showing the use of rivets in the repair of pottery**
This Copeland & Garrett open baking dish from 1833–47 shows
the "Seasons", but its damaged state has devalued it greatly.
£10–20/$15–30

As regards the care of a pottery collection, it is of great importance to preserve the items in the same condition as when they were purchased (except for any necessary cleaning). Keep a detailed record of the items, including the date of purchase, cost, and condition, along with a receipted invoice if you have one. A photographic catalogue is a good method of recording – try photographing each new item in the collection as you acquire it, which is far easier than trying to document a whole collection all at once.

One of the golden rules is to clean each new item as you get it. Examine everything carefully for any sign of restoration, running a finger gently all over the surface of the item; take note of any change in the texture or feel of the glaze. Next, bring the item into a good light – sometimes moving it gently from side to side to let the light bounce off it from different angles can reveal a repair. If you are satisfied that the item is perfect, wash it in warm soapy water using a normal washing up liquid, never a strong household cleaner or bleach – caustic cleaners or bleach may discolour the item or make the glaze flake. A professional restorer, and some dealers, can remove staining using a peroxide solution that draws the stains out. This should

never be tried at home, and is better left to the experts. Peroxide is highly inflammable and can cause burning to the skin. I was cleaning a platter once when it ignited: luckily the platter was not damaged. Some items may have lived in a smoky atmosphere or in a kitchen, and so have become greasy. The best way to clean these is to leave them to soak for a few hours to soften the dirt. Finally wash them gently and dry them with a soft cloth. Unlike fine porcelain, printed pottery was for everyday domestic use and so was more durable.

If you know the item to be restored, wash it very quickly and gently in cool water and pat it dry: do not soak or rub as this may well remove the restoration. An annual clean of the collection is a good idea, and makes a good opportunity for a thorough inspection of everything. A gentle wash is better than dusting. Items that were purchased as restored may show signs of discoloration after several years, especially if the restoration was done before 1990, when the type of chemicals used improved greatly. The materials used prior to this were liable to turn yellow and flake after a time, giving an unpleasant appearance. This process is hastened if the item is displayed in direct sunlight on a windowsill. A good restorer should be able to

▲ **Old, peeling restoration to a jug handle**
The handle was re-applied at some time. Skilful repairs can go unnoticed for a very long time. Copeland, the "Italian" pattern, *c.*1890. **£140–170/$210–255**

▲ **Old, yellowing restoration to the underside of a Spode pierced basket** The whole object needs to be restored again using modern materials that do not discolour with age. In the "Italian" pattern, *c.*1820. **£120–150/$180–225**
**Properly restored £300–350/$450–525**

remove all of this, making the object look pristine, but it would still be a restored item.

There are two basic types of restoration. The first restores the face of the item, allowing the extent of the damage to remain visible on the underside. The second is more deceptive, consisting of a full restoration, completely covering the repairs and damge inside and out. Neither of these methods creates a usable item, however.

Some items of tableware, especially large platters, often show signs of flaking of the glaze on the underside. The cause of this is usually frost damage, caused by storage when damp on the stone floors of the larder or cold room. It is almost impossible to restore this type of damage unless it is limited to a small area, in which case a restorer will seal the flakes to prevent it getting any worse. Damage from bleach gives a similar appearance, but usually with a smell of bleach. Any item which has a purple-coloured stain under the glaze should be viewed with great caution, as this may indicate that bleach was used in an attempt to clean it in the past. There does not seem to be any way of

removing this type of stain from pottery. Brown rust marks from old non-stainless steel cutlery are also very difficult and often impossible to remove.

One of the very early methods of repairing china was the insertion of rivets. A series of small holes was drilled in the pottery, hot lead rivets were inserted along the line of the damage, and when the lead cooled the rivets contracted, pulling the crack together and making a firm repair. The object could still be used after this – the item illustrated as an example of a rivet repair on the previous page still holds liquid. Rivet repairs were still in use in the middle of the twentieth century; china repairers would call on houses at regular intervals to carry out any rivet repairs needed. It is a very skilled process, and few modern restorers like removing them. They are visible only on the underside of the plates and other flatware. Some restorers will restore on the front and leave the original rivets in place – the choice is up to the individual.

# Pottery Marks

The marking of transfer-printed pottery was unusual before the beginning of the nineteenth century: the earliest marks were impressed into the soft biscuit before firing, and few printed marks were used before 1810. Not all factories marked their wares, especially if producing for the export market – many North American importers had a special underglaze mark, as seen on page 37, so that their clients were not aware of the item's country of origin. With the introduction of the McKinley Traffic Acts of 1891, the country of manufacture had to be included in the mark. You can therefore assume that anything marked "England" dates from after 1891, and "Made in England" indicates twentieth-century manufacture – though there are of course exceptions to this rule, as some potters marked their wares with the country even though not obliged to.

A diamond-shaped device containing figures and letters signifies that the item was made in 1842–1883; after this, "Rd. No." ("Registered No.") followed by figures gives the date of manufacture . Use a specialist ceramic marks book to find exact dates (and more examples). Underglaze marks often include the name of the pattern as well as the factory, and small letters or symbols are individual pottery workers' marks – each worker was paid on a "good from the kiln" basis. Caution should be used if an item is marked "Victoria" or "Victorian", especially if the mark is partially obscured, as this is almost certainly a reproduction mark.

▲ A rare printed mark for Stevenson & Williams, 1828.

▲ Copeland & Garrett and "Aesop's Fables" marks, 1833–47.

▲ Thomas Godwin mark for "William Penn Treaty" pattern, 1834–54.

▲ Adams Staffordshire Warranted impressed mark, 1810–25; and "Gracefield Ireland" printed pattern name.

▲ Printed mark for Goodwins & Harris, 1831–8, from the "Metropolitan Scenery" series, showing Woolwich.

▲ Riley printed mark, 1814–28, for the pattern "The Rookery, Surrey", from the "Large Scroll" border series.

▲ A rare Middlesborough Pottery printed mark, 1834–44, for the "Caledonia" pattern.

▲ Printed mark for Edward & George Phillips, 1822–34.

▲ Attributed to John Meir, 1812–36. Luscombe Devon view, from the "Crown, Acorn & Oak Leaf" border series.

▲ A rare impressed mark for Samuel Barker, of the Don Pottery, 1834–93.

▲ Printed mark for "British Flowers" pattern, attributed to John & William Ridgway, 1814–30.

▲ Davenport Stone China printed mark,1805–20.

▲ Printed mark for Ralph Hall, 1822–49. From the "Select Views" series, showing Pains Hill, Surrey.

▲ Printed mark for Thomas & Benjamin Godwin, 1809–34. Showing View of London.

▲ A very rare printed mark from Belle Vue Pottery, Hull, Yorkshire, 1826–41. A very unusual mark and series.

▲ Enoch Wood & Sons, 1818–46. Item shows Lanercost Priory – not previously recorded as being marked as Wood.

▲ Printed mark for J. & W. Ridgway, 1825. City Hall New York, from the "Beauties of America" series.

▲ Printed mark from Copeland period, 1900–70, for the "Italian" pattern.

▲ Printed mark for North East View of Lancaster, from the "Antique Scenery" series, 1825. Maker unknown.

▲ For a view of Pembroke Hall, Cambridge, from the "College Views" series. J. & W. Ridgway, 1820–5.

# Glossary

**Acanthus**
Prickly-leaved plant used extensively in classical decoration

**Arcaded/Arcading**
Semicircular (or "arched") pierced edging found on dessert plates and basket undertrays. Usually painted rather than printed

**Armorial**
Decorated with a family crest or arms

**Ashet**
Term used in Scotland to describe large meat plates

**Backstamp**
The mark on the underside of pottery, giving the maker or pattern name

**Baluster**
Balustrade shape used for vases, jugs, or urns

**Biscuit**
Unglazed pottery that has been fired once

**Body**
The composition of the clay's raw materials excluding glaze, used for various types of pottery

**Border**
The decorative pattern around the edge of an item

**Botanical decoration**
Floral, or plant, decoration copied from accurate engravings

**Bourdaloue**
A boat-shaped toilet receptacle used by ladies when travelling, also known as a coach pot

**Cache Pot**
Term originating in France to describe a container to cover a plain flower pot

**Charger**
Another name for a platter

**Chinoiserie**
A term to describe decoration in the manner of the Chinese, depicting a stylized idea of China, with a European influence

**Clobbering**
Hand-applied enamel on top of the glaze on underglaze printed wares, used to enhance the decoration

**Coaster**
A term sometimes used for a cheese stand

**Cobalt oxide**
The source of the blue used to decorate blue printed pottery

**Coffee can**
A straight-sided cup used for drinking coffee, usually part of a tea set

**Comport**
A shaped serving dish used as part of a dessert service

**Cornucopia**
A decorative motif consisting of a goat's horn overflowing with flowers, fruit, and corn

**Cow Creamer**
A milk jug in the shape of a cow, whose nose forms the spout

**Cradle**
A cheese dish for holding a whole cheese on its side, often called a truckle

**Crazing**
Fine cracks in the glaze that do not penetrate into the body of the pottery

**Creamer**
A small jug used for serving milk or cream

**Cup plate**
A small plate from a tea service, used to hold the cup after the tea was poured into the saucer for drinking. This practice was quite acceptable in the first half of the nineteenth century

**Dessertware**
Items from a dessert service, usually of a more decorative shape than other dinnerware

**Drainer**
A flat pierced plate that fits into a platter to drain juices from meat or fish; may also be called a mazarine

**Enamel**
A pigment used in the hand-painting of china over the glaze

**Engraver**
The skilled worker who engraves the copper plate from which the pattern is transferred

**Ewer**
A large jug used for water, also known as a pitcher

**Fettling**
The removal by hand of blemishes from the unfired clay

**Finial**
The knob or handle on a lid

**Firing**
The baking of the clay at various stages in the manufacturing process

**Flatware**
Plates, soup plates, and other flat table wares

**Flow or Flown blue**
Effect when the colour is allowed to flow from the design, giving a smudged appearance, caused by the addition of chemicals in the second firing

**Frog mug**
A mug with a frog and often a newt painted in the inside in bright-coloured enamels, visible only after the liquid was drunk – the origin of the phrase, "drunk as a newt"

**Gadrooned edge or Gadrooning**
A raised decorative edge, often in white, introduced on pottery around 1820

**Garniture**
A set of usually three vases or urns for decoration

**Gilding**
Decoration using applied gold or gold leaf

**Glaze**
A glass-like mixture applied to the item before the final firing giving, a hard glossy finish

**Good from oven (or kiln)**
The system by which pottery workers were paid: per item that was perfect after firing; each potter would have his own mark

**Harlequin**
A term used to describe a mixture of items of different patterns or colours

**Hollow-ware**
Cups, jugs, bowls etc. – as opposed to flatware

**Ironstone**
The stone china patented by Mason

**Loving cup**
A two-handled mug often given as a love or marriage token

**Marriage Pot**
A two-handled chamber pot often given to a couple to mark their marriage

**Milsey**
A small round, flat item with holes used for straining milk

**Mould**
Used to shape items of hollow-ware before firing

**Nankin**
An inner border, usually Oriental in style

**Pap feeder**
A small boat-shaped item used to feed babies with pap or warm milk, or invalids with milk and alcohol

**Pearlware**
White earthenware with a blue added to the glaze, giving a pearl-like appearance and often leaving blue around the foot-rims.

**Pilgrim flask**
A flat circular or oval flask used for carrying liquids when travelling

**Saggar or Sagger**
Clay container for wares in which the pottery is stacked for firing in the kiln

**Salt cellar**
Small, circular or oval, footed dish used for salt

**Sheet pattern**
A repetitive all-over decoration of pottery giving the appearance of wallpaper

**Smokers' set**
A fitted column containing a tobacco jar, candle, and spitoon, the complexity of which varies

**Spill vase**
A vase for holding small rolls or twists of paper, or slips of wood ("spills") used for lighting a fire, a pipe, etc.

**Stilt marks**
Pinhead-sized marks on the edges of pottery caused by the pieces of clay used to separate the items during firing

**Stringing**
A narrow border decoration at either the outer or inner edge of the border

**Sucrier**
A small covered or open basin for serving sugar

**Syllabub**
A dessert made from cream or milk, whipped to thicken it

**Tea bowl**
A handleless cup

**Tig or Tyg**
A mug with three handles

**Transfer printing**
The process of decorating using transfers, as opposed to painting

**Transitional**
Decoration in the Chinese style with a more European influence, from the early nineteenth century

**Treacle jar**
A lidded screw-top item, usually with a handle, for storing treacle

**Tunnel kiln**
A modern, electrically operated oven which replaced the kiln. As the pots pass through on a trolley, the temperature increases, decreasing near the end and so reducing the risk of pottery shrinkage

**Underglaze**
Decoration applied under the glaze

**Undertray**
Matching under-dish for tureens or baskets

**Veilleuse**
A small heater with a night light to keep gruel or tea warm

**Vitrescent China**
Term used to describe a particularly hard and glass-like glaze

**Waisted**
Having a smaller diameter at the "waist" than at the top or bottom

**Well-and-tree**
Term used to describe a large meat platter with grooves often in the shape of tree branches running into a well, where the meat juices and fat would collect; also known as a venison dish

# Further Reading

## Blue & White Pottery

**Arman, David & Linda**
*Historical Staffordshire: An Illustrated Check List*
(Arman Enterprises, 1975)

**Copeland, Robert**
*Spode's Willow Pattern & Other Designs After the Chinese* (Studio Vista, 1980)

**Copeland, Robert**
*Blue & White Transfer-Printed Pottery*
(Shire Publications, 1998)

**Coysh, A. W.**
*Blue & White Transferware 1780–1840*
(David & Charles, 1970)

**Coysh, A. W.**
*Blue Printed earthenware 1800–1850*
(David & Charles, 1972)

**Coysh, A.W. & Henrywood, R.K.**
*The Dictionary of Blue & White Printed Pottery, Volumes I & II* (Antique Collectors' Club, 1982, 1989)

**Drakard, David; & Holdaway, Paul**
*Spode Printed Ware* (Longman Higher Education, 1983; Antique Collectors' Club, 2002)

**Gaston, Mary F.**
*Blue Willow Identification & Value Guide*
(Collector Books, 2003)

**Haines Halsey, R. T.**
*Pictures of Early New York on Dark Blue Staffordshire Pottery (Together with Pictures of Boston & New England, Philadelphia, the South and West)*
(Dover Publications, 1974)

**Larsen, Ellouise B.**
*American Historical Views on Staffordshire China*
(Dover Publications, 1975, 1976)

**Little, W.**
*Staffordshire Blue* (B. T. Batsford, 1969, 1988)

**Neale, Gillian**
*Blue & White Pottery, A Collector's Guide*
(Miller's, 2000)

**Priestman, Geoffrey H.**
*An Illustrated Guide to Minton Printed Pottery 1796–1836* (Endcliffe Press, 2001)

**Snyder, Jeffrey**
*Fascinating Flow Blue* (Schiffer Publishing, 1997)
(Snyder has written several books on Flow Blue)

**Snyder, Jeffrey**
*Historical Staffordshire American Patriots & Views, A Schiffer Book for Collectors* (Schiffer Publishing, 1995)

**Williams, Sydney B.**
*Antique Blue & White Spode* (B. T. Batsford, 1987)

## Other Printed Pottery

**Furniss, David A., et al**
*Adams Ceramics: Staffordshire Potters & Pots*
(Schiffer Publishing, 1999)

**Godden, Geoffrey A.**
*Godden's Guide to Mason's China and the Ironstone Wares* (Antique Collectors' Club, 1980)

**Griffin, John**
*Don Pottery Pattern Book*
(Doncaster Library Service, 1983)

**Henrywood, R. K.**
*An Illustrated Guide to British Jugs*
(Swan Hill Press, 1997)

**Henrywood, R. K.**
*Staffordshire Potters 1781–1900*
(Antique Collectors' Club, 2003)

**Jewitt, Llewellyn**
*The Ceramic Art of Great Britain*
(Barrie & Jenkins, 1972)

**Lewis, Griselda**
*Collectors' History of English Pottery*
(Antique Collectors' Club, 1985)

**Savage, George & Newman, Harold**
*An Illustrated Dictionary of Ceramics*
(Thames & Hudson, 1986)

**Snyder, Jeffrey**
*Romantic Staffordshire* (Schiffer Publishing, 1997)

**Whiter, Leonard**
*Spode* (Barrie & Jenkins, 1970)

**Williams, Petra**
*Staffordshire Romantic Transfer Patterns: Cup Plates and Early Victorian China* (Fountain House East, 1978)

## Pottery Marks

**Copeland, Robert**
*Spode & Copeland Marks* (Studio Vista, 1993)

**Godden, Geoffrey A.**
*Encyclopaedia of British Pottery & Porcelain Marks*
(Hutchinson, 1987)

# Index

Page numbers in **bold** refer to main entries, those in *italic* refer to illustrations

## A

"Abbey" pattern 41, 142
"Abbey Ruins" pattern 139
"Absalom's Pillar" series (Wedgwood) 57, 82
"Acorn & Oak Leaf" border series (Stevenson) 34
Adams
    animals & birds 60
    border series designs *34*, 44–5, 91
    city & town designs *34, 35,* 50, 91
    dinnerware *34–5, 90,* 91
    export ware 34, *35,* 91
    marks 34, 91, *149*
    other colours used 140–1
    tea kettles *106*
"Aesop's Fables" series (Spode) 25, *60,* 61, 138, *142,* 143
Alcock, Samuel *128*
"Angry Lion" pattern 60
"Angus Seats" series (Ridgway) 84
animals *7,* 18, *20,* 36, **58–61**
    *see also individual factories; sporting subjects*
"Antelope" pattern (Jackson) 141
"Antique Scenery" series *9,* 49, *127,* 150
"Arabesque" pattern (Minton) 139
arcading *33,* 98–9
"Arched Bridge" pattern *134*
"Archery" pattern (Herculaneum) 142
"Arctic Scenery" series 36, 60
Argyles *129,* 130
armorial designs 19, 34, **66–9,** 88
    *see also individual factories*
"Arms of America" series (Mayer) 19, 34
Ashworth Brothers 93
"Asiatic Pheasants" pattern 41, 63
"Asiatic Plants" pattern *139*
asparagus servers 128

## B

"Bacchus" pattern *122*
backstamps *31, 61,* 71, 90, 91
Baggerley & Ball 65
baking dishes *51, 58,* 96, *147*
"Bamboo & Fence" pattern 82, *115*

"Bamboo & Vase" pattern (Minton) *80*
Barker, Samuel *16, 150*
"Basket" pattern (Minton) 72, 80
baskets *17, 29, 66, 78,* 98, *99, 148*
"Beaded Frame" series (Mason) *50,* 51, *92*
"Beauties of America" series (Ridgway) 19, 34, *35,* 54, 85, *150*
"Bee Catcher" pattern *104*
"Beehive & Vase" pattern (Stevenson & Williams) *63*
"Beehive" pattern 140
"Beemaster" pattern 18, *25*
Bell 65, 74
Belle Vue Pottery 48, *48–9, 150*
"Belzoni" pattern (Wood) 90–1
"Benevolent Cottagers" (Minton) 80–1
"Bewick Stag" pattern (Minton) 80
"Bird Chinoiserie" pattern (Adams) *90,* 91
bird feeders *128,* 129
birds 41, **62–3,** 73, 82, *90,* 91, 143
"Birds & Flowers" pattern *111, 112*
"Bird's Nest" pattern 62, *63,* 75
"Bisham Abbey" pattern (Davenport) *26,* 86
black transferware 19, 25, 61, 143
"Blind Boy" pattern (Ridgway) 84
"Blossom" pattern (Spode) 78, *79, 120*
"Blue Claude" pattern (Wedgwood) 82
"Blue Marble" pattern (Minton) *122*
"Blue Pheasants" pattern (Mason) 63
"Blue Rose" border series (Wedgwood) 82
"Blue Rose" pattern (Spode) 71, *109,* 143
"Bluebell" border series 44, 91
borders *16,* 27, *30,* 60, 67, 76
    *see also individual names*
"Boston State House" pattern (Rogers) 19, 34, 54, 89
"Botanical Groups" pattern (Minton) 72, 81
"Botanical" pattern *7,* 18, *22,* 70, 71, 72, 81, 138
"Botanical Vase" pattern (Minton) 72, 81
Bovey Tracey Pottery 68, *134*
bowls 89
    armorial designs 68
    fruit 28, *30,* 62, 98
    punchbowls *24*
    salad *26, 95,* 96
    tea *63, 104, 108*

    *see also* dog bowls; toiletware
"Bowpot" pattern (Spode) 78
"Boy on Buffalo" pattern *see* "Buffalo" pattern
"The Boy Piping" pattern *95*
Boyle, Zachariah 30, *31*
Brameld Pottery 72–3, 75, *96*
breakfast ware 100
"Bridge of Lucano" pattern 29, 74, 77
"Bridgeless Willow" pattern (Davenport) *26,* 86
"Britannia" pattern (Rogers) 89
"British Birds" series 143
"British Flowers" pattern 71, *73,* 84, *103, 136,* 138
"British Flowers" series (Ridgway) *19,* 71–2, *73, 150*
"British History" series (Jones) 18–19, 54, *55*
"British Palaces" series (Stevenson) 143
"British Views" series (Henshall) 75, *97*
"Broseley" pattern 26, *103, 117*
brown transferware 19, *23,* 25, 70, 85, 142–3
"Buddleia" pattern (Spode) 76
"Buffalo" pattern 16, *17, 27,* 76
butter dishes 120, *121,* 128, *131*
buying blue & white **20–2**
"Byron's Views" series 25, *110,* 138

## C

"Caledonia" pattern (Middlesborough) *23, 149*
"Camel & Giraffe" pattern (Minton) 80
"Camel" pattern (Rogers) 57, 88
"Camilla" pattern 138, *139*
candlesticks & snuffer trays *76, 82, 85*
"Canova" pattern (Mayer) 142
"Canton Views" pattern (Hamilton) 27
"Caramanian" series (Spode) *7, 10,* 16–17, 56, *76, 115, 117,* 143
Carey, Thomas & John 18, 50, 93
caring for blue & white 43, 45, 51, *113,* **147–8**
"Carra" pattern *130*
"Castle & Bridge" pattern (Henshall) *17*
"Castle Gateway" pattern (Minton) 80
"Castle of Rocheforte" pattern (Brameld) 75
"Castle" pattern *28,* 74, 77
"Cathedral" series (Carey) 18, 50
cathedrals & abbeys *7, 8, 9,* 18, *46–7, 48*

"Cattle & River" pattern
(Heathcote) 96
Cauldon *40*
Challinor, Edward 30, *31*, 56–7, *64*,
*123, 126*
"Chantilly Sprig" pattern (Spode)
*70, 78*
chargers *19, 95*
cheese dishes & stands *29, 36, 41,*
**118–21**
"Chess Players" pattern 140
"Chinese Bird" pattern (Adams)
*90, 91*
"Chinese Dragons" pattern
(Mason) *93*
"Chinese Flowers" pattern (Spode)
*78*
"Chinese Garden" pattern 80, 82
Chinese influence 6, 14, *15,* 16,
**26–7,** 74 *see also individual
factories*; Oriental influence
"Chinese Landscape" pattern
(Wedgwood) 82
"Chinese Marine" pattern
(Minton) 40, 81, *137*
"Chinese of Rank" pattern 77, *122*
"Chinese Temple" pattern
(Ridgway) 85
"Chinese Trophies" pattern 27
"Chinese Vase" pattern
(Wedgwood) 82
"Chinoiserie High Bridge" pattern
*27, 97*
"Chinoiserie Ruins" pattern 16, 84,
86, *117*
chocolate pots & cups 108–9, *131*
cities & towns 7, *34,* 35, *46,* **50–3**
*see also individual factories*
"Cities & Towns" series (Harvey) 53
Clementson *113*
Clews 28, 35, *36,* 44–5, 91, *118,* 142
clobbering *50,* 51, 79, *92, 98, 99*
clubs 23, *103, 107*
Clyde Pottery 74, *135*
"Clyde Scenery" series (Jackson) 141
coffee pots & cans *27, 93,* 105–6, *106*
collections **6–8, 20–5,** *43, 61,* 74
"College" series (Mason) *92,* 93
"College Views" series (Ridgway)
19, 52, 84, *150*
coloured transferware 19, 25, *36, 61,*
**138–43** *see also individual colours*
"Columbus" series (Adams) 140
commemorative ware *54,* 55
comports 28, *42–3, 53, 68, 73,* 98
condition 94–5, 99, 101, 102, 106,
108, 111, 126–7
Copeland & Garrett (later
Copeland) 25, *61,* 67, 71, 76, 138,
*147, 149*
Copeland (prev Spode)
armorial designs *66,* 67, 68

cheese dishes & stands *119,* 121
classical subjects *107*
dinnerware *64–5, 66*
egg cups *103*
floral designs 71
flow blue designs *38*
marks *150*
other colours used *138, 139,* 141
pickle dishes 125
sporting subjects *64,* 65
toiletware 68, *136*
tureens & stands *138, 139*
copies 28, 30–1, 74, 82–3
copper plates 9–10, *11,* 12
"Corinthian" pattern (Minton) 81
Cork & Edge 93, *141*
"Cornucopia" border series
(Davenport) 75
"Cottages & Cart" pattern (Minton)
81
"Country Scene" pattern (Spode) 77
cow creamers 108
"Cowman" pattern (Ridgway) 84
"Cracked Ice" pattern (Spode) 78
"Crane" pattern (Wedgwood) 82
"Crown, Acorn, & Oak Leaf" border series (Meir) 18, *42–3, 150*
"Cupid" series (Wood) 90
cups & saucers *29, 59, 62, 63,* 104–5,
*108, 113*
"Curling Palm" pattern (Ridgway)
84
custard cups *8, 64, 75,* 98

**D**

"Daffodil" pattern (Lane End) 73
"Dagger" pattern (Spode) *68*
"Dahlia" pattern (Minton) 72
"Daisy & Bead" pattern (Spode) 71,
78–9
"Daisy" pattern (Spode) 78
Davenport
Chinese influence 16, 26, 86
dinnerware *75, 86,* 97
dishes *26,* 87
export ware 37, *75,* 86
floral designs 87
landscapes 86, 87
marks *150*
miniature china *112*
other colours used 138–9
stone china 93, *150*
supper sets 16
toiletware 87
tureens & stands *115*
Dawson Pottery 62, 75
Deakin & Bailey 140, *141*
"Demon's Egypt" pattern (Maling)
75
dessertware **98–9,** 114–15
*see also* baskets; comports; dishes

dinnerware **94–7** *see also* plates;
platters; tureens
dishes
dessert *18, 30, 79,* 87
*see also* comports
sweetmeat *76, 88,* 98, *102*
warming *22*
*see also* baking dishes; cheese
dishes; pickle dishes; supper sets
displaying blue & white 22, 24, 45,
101–2, 116–17, 127, **144–5**
dog bowls *18, 39, 41,* 129
"Domed Building" pattern
(Minton) 81
Don Pottery 16, 25, 75, *131, 150*
"Don Quixote" pattern (Brameld) 75
"Dove" pattern (Minton) *124*
"Dr Syntax" series (Clews) 35, *36*
"Dragons" pattern (Mason) *93*
drainers & strainers 95, 96, **116–17,**
*139*
"Drama" series (Rogers) 89
"Dresden" pattern (Minton) 72
"Durham Ox" series 7, *18, 20,* 59, 74

**E**

"Eastern Street Scene" pattern
(Riley) 88
edges *15,* 17, *33,* 63, *73,* 85, *109*
egg cups/stands 100, *101,* 103
"Elephant" pattern 16, 58, 74, 88
Elkin & Knight 51, 88
"English Cities" series (Wood) 90
English country houses 7, 32–3,
*42–3, 75,* 84, *85,* 125
"English Scenery" series (Minton) 81
"English Sprays" pattern (Spode)
71, *138*
"English Views" series (Rogers) 141
"Equestrian" pattern *142*
"Europa" pattern (Riley) 88
"Exotic Birds" pattern *128*
export ware 19, **34–7,** 44, 45, 51, 140,
141, 142 *see also individual factories*
eye baths *135,* 137

**F**

"Fallow Deer" pattern 81, 83, 88, *117*
"Farm" pattern (Metheven) *110*
"Farmyard Scene" pattern
(Minton) 81
feeding bottles & cups 110–11
"Feeding the Chickens" pattern
(Riley) 89
"Feeding the Turkeys" pattern
*140,* 141
Fell, Thomas 109
"Fence" pattern (Spode) 78
"Ferns" pattern *128*
"Ferrara" pattern (Wedgwood) 83

"Field Sports" series (Copeland) 64, *65*, *138*, 139
"Filigree" pattern *7*, 71, 72, *78*, 81, *100*, *126*
"Fisherman" series 80, 86, 91
"Fitzhugh" pattern (Spode) *68*
flasks *25*, 130, *131*
"Flora" pattern 81, *133*
"Floral Basket" pattern 66, *67*, *126*
floral designs *7*, 35, *70–3*
  *see also* individual factories
"Floral" pattern (Spode) 70–1, *73*, 138
"Floral Sprays" pattern (Spode) *139*
"Floral Vase" pattern (Minton) 72, *80*, *101*
"Florentine" pattern (Minton) 72, 81
flow blue 14, 23, **38–9**
"Flower Cross" pattern (Spode) 78
"Flowers & Leaves" border series (Adams) *34*, 91
"Flying Pennant" pattern (Spode) 16, *17*, *26*, 76, *131*
"Foliage" border series 44–5
"Forest Landscape" pattern (Spode) *26–7*
"Fountain" pattern 91, *140*
"French Birds" pattern (Spode) *79*
"French Chateaux" pattern (Hall) 141
"French" series (Wood) 37, 90
"Fruit & Flowers" pattern 73, 78
furniture lifters 129, *130*

**G**

gadrooning 63, 73, 79, 85, *109*
"Gamekeeper" pattern (Hackwood) 18, 64–5
garden seats 29, *38*
"Gem" pattern (Jamieson) *10*
"Genevese" pattern (Minton) 40–1, *132*
"Geranium" pattern (Spode) 68–9, 71
"Giraffe" pattern (Ridgway) 142
"Girl Musician" pattern (Riley) 88
glazing 10, 13, 39, 67
"Gloucester" pattern (Spode) 78
Godwin, Thomas & Benjamin 37, 50, 55, 57, 142, *149*, *150*
"The Goldfinch" pattern 62, *104*
Goodwin, Bridgewood, & Orton 73
Goodwin & Harris 50, *51*, 65, *149*
"Gothic Castle" pattern (Spode) 77
"Grapevine" border series (Wood) 18, 48, 51, 90
"Grasshopper" pattern (Spode) 27, 77
gravy boats 96
"Grazing Rabbits" pattern 18, 58–9
"Grecian" pattern (Wood) 90
"Greek" pattern 79, *98*, *101*, *102*, 115
green transferware 19, 25, 61, 64, 71, **138–9**
"Group" pattern (Spode) 27, 71, *98*, *100*, *124*

**H**

Hackwood 18, 64–5
Hall, John 59–60
Hall, Ralph *36*, 50, 141, *150*
Hamilton 27, 33
"Harvest Scenery" pattern 141
Harvey 51, 53
hash dishes 96, 115
"Hawthornden" pattern *119*
Heath *15*
Heathcote 96
Henshall *17*, 75, 97
Herculaneum Pottery 16, 17, 27, 57, 61, 65, *101*, 142
"Hermit" pattern (Minton) 16, 26, 80
"Hibiscus" pattern (Wedgwood) 18, 70
Hicks & Meigh 67, 73, *92*, *93*, *109*, 124
historical subjects 18–19, 34, **54–5**, 90
history of blue & white **14–19**
Holland, J. *130*
honey pots 70
"Honeysuckle & Parsley" pattern (Spode) 71, 78
"Humphrey's Clock" series (Ridgway) 111, 113
"Hundred Antiquities" pattern 27

**I**

"Improved Wild Rose" pattern 32
"India Flowers" pattern (Ridgway) 72
"India" series (Herculaneum) 17, 57
"Indian Sporting" series (Spode) 6–7, 17, 56, 58, 64, 79
"Indian Views" series (Godwin) 57
inkwells 128
invalid feeders *136*, 137
"Irish Scenery" series (Carey) 18
ironstone china 14, 18, 50, 63, 67, **92–3**, 93
"Italian Building" pattern (Hall) 141
"Italian Church" pattern (Spode) 29, 78
"Italian Flower Garden" pattern (Ridgway) *84*, 85
Italian influence 7, 17, **28–31**, 40
  *see also* Spode
"Italian" pattern (others) 30–1, 40, 74, *119*, 121, *125*, *148*, *150*
"Italian" pattern (Spode) 28–9, 77, *94*, *99*, *120*, *131*, 137
"Italian Ruins" pattern (Minton) 81

**J**

Jackson 35, 36, 141, 142
Jamieson *10*
"Japan" pattern (Spode) *103*
"Jasmine" pattern (Spode) 66, 69, 71, *109*
Jones, George 18–19, 41, 54, *55*, 67

jugs *8*, *17*, 24–5, *54*, **122–3**
  handles 122, 123, *148*
  milk & cream *78*, 108, *122*
  in other colours *139*, *140*
  for punch 122, 123
  puzzle *32*, 74, *81*, 122
  water *52*, *123*, 139
  *see also* toiletware

**K**

Keeling *24*
"Kirk" pattern (Minton) 80
knife rests *17*, *95*, 97

**L**

labels 146
"Lace Border" series 35–6, 72, *134*
"Ladies of Llangollen" pattern (Swansea) 74
"Lakeside Meeting" pattern (Keeling) 24
Lakin, Thomas 29, 78
"Large Scroll" border series (Riley) 88, *89*, *149*
"Lattice Scroll" pattern (Spode) 78
"Lazuli" pattern (Swansea) 38
"Leaf" pattern 72, 78
Leeds Pottery *6*, 124
"Lily" pattern 78, 80
"Lion Antique" pattern *122*
"Lion" pattern (Adams) 60
London scenes *34*, 35, *46*, **50–1**, 83
"London Views" series (Wood) 35, 50–1, 90
"Long Bridge" pattern *6*, 15, 76
"Long Eliza" pattern (Spode) *8*, 77, *121*
"Lorraine" pattern (Adams) 91
"Lotus" pattern *70*
"Love Chase" pattern *107*
Lowndes & Beech *111*
"Lyre" pattern (Spode) 78, *105*

**M**

Maling 75
"Mandarin Opaque" pattern (Ridgway) 84
manufacture of blue & white **9–13**, 74–5
"Marble" pattern (Spode) 78
Mare *30*, *31*
marks 34–5, 38, 63, 92, 93, **149–50**
  *see also* backstamps; individual factories
Mason family 14, *50*, 51, 55, 92, 141, 142
Mason's ironstone 14, 63, 92–3
mauve transferware 113, *140*
Mayer, Thomas 19, 34, 140
"Maypole" pattern (Minton) 81
"Medallion Portrait" series

(Stevenson) 54
medical items 68, *79*, 87, 111–12, *135*, **136–7**
Meigh family 60, 67, 93
Meir, John 18, 42–3, *110*, *132*, *150*
menu holders *15*
Metheven, David *110*, 113
"Metropolitan Scenery" series (Goodwin & Harris) 50, *51*, *149*
Middlesborough Pottery *23*, *149*
"Milkmaid" pattern (Spode) 59, 77, *109*
miniature china 25, *106*, *110*, **112–14**, 140, *141*, 142–3
*see also* individual factories
Minton
animals & birds 62–3, 80
Chinese influence 16, 26, 80
egg cups *101*
floral designs 7, 18, 72, 80, 81, *101*
jugs *81*
later patterns 40–1
marks 72, 81
miniature china 80, 81, 112–13
other colours used 139, 140, 142
pickle dishes *124*, 125
platters *81*
rural scenes 80–1
toiletware 41, *72*, 80, *123*, 132–3, *134*, *137*, 145
"Willow" pattern 80
"Minton Miniatures" series (Minton) 81, 112–13
"Mogul Scenery" (Mayer) 140
"Monk's Rock" series (Minton) 80
"Monopteros" pattern (Rogers) 57, 88
"Months" series (Wedgwood) 83
"Mosque & Fisherman" pattern (Davenport) 87
mugs 7, *55*, 68, 81
"Musicians" pattern (Spode) *76*, 77
"Musketeer" pattern (Rogers) 57, 88
mustard pots 97

**N**

"Named Italian Views" series 75, *131*
"Nankin" pattern (Spode) 69
"The Napoleon" series (Mason) 55, 141, 142
"Net" pattern 16, *18*, 27, 76–7, 84, *98*
"Nuneham Courtenay" pattern 32–3, *125*
nursery china 43, 61, 94, **110–12**, 140, *142*, 143

**O**

ointment pots 68, *79*
"Olympic Games" pattern (Mayer) 142

"Opium Smokers" pattern (Mason) 92
orange transferware 143
"Oriental Birds" pattern 62, 63, 85, 142
"Oriental Flower Garden" (Goodwin, Bridgewood, & Orton) 73
Oriental influence 6–7, *10*, 16–17, **56–7** *see also* Chinese influence; *individual factories*
"Oriental" series (Ridgway) 85
"Oriental Sports" series (Challinor) 56–7, *64*, 127
"Ornithological Birds" series 62–3
"Osterley Park" pattern (Ridgway) 50
"Ottoman Empire" series (Ridgway) 17, 57
oyster pans *94*, 96–7

**P**

pails *31*, *91*, 97, 98, *132*, 133–4
"Panorama" pattern *145*
pap feeders 111
"Parasol & Figure" design (Spode) *14*
"Park Scenery" pattern (Phillips) *19*
"Parroquet" pattern (Brameld) 73
"Parrot" border (Ridgway) 17
"Passion Flower" border series 50
patty pans 102
"Peony" pattern (Wedgwood) 18, 70, 82, *105*
"Peplow" pattern (Spode) 78
pepper pots 97
Phillips, Edward & George *19*, 62, *63*, 84–5, 142
"Philosopher" pattern (Hamilton) 33
pickle dishes 7, *26*, 43, *74*, 98, 102, **124–5**
"Picturesque Scenery" series (Hall) 50
"Pier Fishing" pattern (Adams) *35*
"Pineapple" border series 47
"Pink Camilla" pattern (Copeland) 141
"Pink Tower" pattern (Copeland) 141
pink transferware 29, 140–1
"Pinwheel" pattern (Minton) 80
plate lifters *82*
plates
advertising *20*
animals & birds 7, 60–1, 62, 63, 74
armorial designs 67, 68–9
cheese *47*, 62, *73*, *84*, *141*
Chinese influence *14*, 27, 86, *90*
city & town views 52
dessert *33*, 45, 47, 62, 68, 73, 89
dinner *14*, 47, 95, 97
edges *15*, 98–9

for export *34–7*
floral designs *71–2*, 73
miniature 43, 61, *112*, 141
nursery 113
Oriental influence 14, 56, 57
in other colours 141, 142–3
rural scenes *25*, *33*, 95
sandwich 28
serial patterns *33*, *42*, *43*, *44–9*
sizes 94
sporting subjects *64–5*
warming 137
*see also* chargers; platters; soup plates
platters
animals & birds 20, *58*, *60*, 88
cathedrals and abbeys 9
Chinese influence 6, *15*, 82
English scenes 75, *81*, *84*, 85–6, 88
for fish 95–6
historical subjects 54
Italian influence *30*
London views 50–1, *90*
Oriental influence *10*, 56, 57
in other colours *142*
rural scenes 96
serial patterns 46–7, *48*, *49*, *86*, 96
sizes 95
"Pomeriana" series (Ridgway) 141, *142*
Pountney & Allies 30, *31*, 51, *52*, 53
Pountney & Co. 68
Pountney & Goldney 30, *31*, 89
promotional ware 28, 41
"Prunus" pattern (Spode) 78
puce transferware *25*, *55*, 140
"Pultney Bridge, Bath" design (Swansea) 53, 74

**Q**

"Quadrupeds" series 36, 59–60

**R**

"Ravena" pattern *135*
"Regent's Park" series (Adams) *34*, 35, 50, 91
"Reindeer" pattern (Heath) *15*
reproductions 19, 39, 41, 60
restoration 17, 39, 45, 108, 147–8
"Returning Woodman" pattern (Brameld) 75, *96*
"Rhine Views" series (Davenport) 87
Ridgway
animals & birds *58*, 63, 85
Chinese influence 27, 84
city & town designs 19, 50, *52*, 84
collecting 85
dessertware 73
Dickensian scenes 111, 113
dinnerware *19*, *35*, *52*, *57*, *71*,

*84, 85*
export ware 19, 34, *35,* 54, 85
feeding bottles *111*
floral designs *19,* 71–2, *73,* 84–5
historical subjects 54
jugs *84*
marks 72, *150*
Oriental influence 17, 57, 85
other colours used 140, 141
rural scenes *58,* 84
Riley, John & Richard 17, *56,* 57, 66–7, 88, *89, 149*
"River Thames" series (Pountney & Allies) 51
Robinson, Wood, & Brownfield *58,* 60
"Rock Cartouche" series (Elkin & Knight) 51, 88
Rogers
   animals & birds 16, *36,* 57, 58, 88
   dinnerware *57,* 88
   dishes *88*
   drainers & strainers *117*
   European landscapes 89
   export ware 19, 34, 54, 89
   floral designs 73
   historical subjects 54
   marks *37*
   Oriental influence 57, 88
   other colours used 141
   rural scenes 88–9
   theatrical scenes 89
   toiletware *36, 133*
"Rogers Views" series (Rogers) 88–9
"Roman" pattern (Minton) 80
"Rome" pattern (Spode) 29, 77, 78
"Royal Cottage" pattern (Till) *116*
"Ruined Abbey" pattern (Minton) 80
"Rural Scenery" series *58,* 138–9
rural scenes 7, 18, *25,* 32–3, 58–9, 75, *95*–6 *see also individual factories*
"Rural Village" pattern 33
"Russian Palace" pattern *127*
"Rustic Scenes" series (Davenport) 86

**S**
salt cellars & spoons *66,* 97, *112*
samples *113*
"Scott's Illustrations" series (Davenport) 87
"Scripture" series (Wood) 90
"The Sea" series (Adams) 140–1
"Seasons" series 83, *106,* 141, *147*
"Select Views" series (Hall) *36, 150*
"Semi-China Warranted" series (Stevenson) *58,* 59, *94, 95*
serial patterns 17–18, 49
   *see also individual names*
Sewell & Fell 75
Shaw, Anthony 37, 54, 141, 142

sheet patterns 18, 38–9, 71, 73, *87*
"Shell" border series (Wood) 90
"Shepherdess" pattern (Spode) 77
Smith, William 59, 109, *122*
smoking equipment *23, 86,* 131
soup plates *19,* 22, 27, *44, 45, 49,* 94, 96
"South American Sports" series 65
Southwick Pottery 109
spittoons *136,* 137
Spode (later Copeland)
   animals & birds 16, 25, 58, 59, *60,* 61, *62,* 79, *79*
   armorial designs *66,* 68–9, 71
   bowls *26, 30*
   cheese dishes & stands *29, 41,* 118, *120*–1
   Chinese influence *14,* 16, 26–7, 76–7
   classical subjects 79, *98, 101, 102, 107, 115*
   collecting 7, 23, 24, 74, 76, 79
   copies 28, 30–1, 74
   dessertware *8, 17,* 28–9, *68, 75, 78*–9, *98*–9
   dinnerware *94 see also* plates
   dishes *18,* 22, 28–30, *62, 66, 75, 76, 79*
   drainers & strainers *117, 139*
   floral designs 7, 18, 68–9, *70,*–1, 78–9
   Italian influence 17, 28–9, 40, 77–8
   jugs *78*
   later patterns 40, 41
   limited editions 41
   marks *31,* 77, 78
   medical items *68, 79,* 135, *136*
   miniature china 71, 79, 112, *113*
   Oriental influence 16–17, 56, 79
   other colours used 138, *139,* 142, 143
   pickle dishes *7,* 124
   plates & platters *10, 14,* 22, 27, *60*–1, *69,* 71, *73*
   rural scenes 59, 77
   sporting subjects 6–7, 17, 56, 58, 64, 79
   stone china *14,* 27, 93
   supper sets 100–1, *102*
   tea wares *29, 105,* 107–9
   toiletware *133,* 135, *136, 137*
   tureens & stands *60,* 61, *73,* 77, *115*
   "Willow" pattern 15, 26, 76, *135*
spoon rests *43*
spoons & ladles 96, 97, *112,* 114, **126**–7
"Sporting" series (Wood) *8,* 36, 64, 65, 90
sporting subjects **64**–5, 86, *138,* 139
   *see also individual factories*
"Springer Spaniel" pattern (Stevenson) 64

"Stafford Gallery" series (Ridgway) 85
"Starflower" pattern (Spode) 79
Stevenson
   animals & birds *58,* 59, 62–3, 64
   Chinese influence 27
   coffee pots 27
   dinnerware *58, 64, 94, 95,* 96
   English scenes 96
   export ware 34, *35*–6
   historical subjects 54
   other colours used 142, 143
   rural scenes *94, 95*
   sporting subjects 64
Stevenson & Williams *63, 149*
stone china 14, 27, 93
"Strawflower" pattern (Spode) 71
Stubbs 30, *31,* 34
"Stylised Flowers" (Goodwin, Bridgewood, & Orton) 73
sugar boxes 108, *109*
"Sunflower" pattern (Spode) 71
supper sets *16, 59,* 100–2
Swansea 28, 38, 53, 58, 65, 74, *118, 122,* 140
"Sweet Pea" pattern (Brameld) 72–3

**T**
"Tea Party" pattern 75, 109
tea wares 26, *59, 63,* 78, 81, **104**–**9**
   *see also* chocolate; coffee
teapots & stands 14, *16, 105,* 106–7
"Temple Landscape" pattern *129*
"Temple" pattern 26, *128*
"Tendril" pattern (Adams) 73
"Texian Campaign" series (Shaw) 37, 54, 141, 142
"The Crossing" pattern 7
"Tiber" pattern (Spode) 29, 77, 78
Till, Thomas *116*
toiletware **132**–**6**
   bedpans *110,* 136
   bidets *133,* 135
   chamber/vomit pots 97, *134,* 135–6, *137*
   footbaths 72, *80, 132,* 134–5
   jugs & ewers *36, 38, 53, 70, 84, 123,* 132, 133
   leg baths 135, *137*
   pails *91, 132,* 133–4
   soap dishes & boxes *39,* 131, 132, 133
   toilet boxes *52, 80,* 132
   toothbrush head covers 130–1
   washbowls *36, 53, 80,* 132–3, *145*
   water closets & urinals 29, *87, 134, 135,* 136
"Tower" pattern (Copeland) 29, *40,* 68, 121
"Tower" pattern (Spode) *18,* 22, 28–9, *79, 99,* 110, 112, *133,* 136